True Story

of

PROMISING

FORECAST

a

Miracle Rescue at Sea

Written by

Daniel David Jones

Co-authored by

Arthur J. Hill

D0871678

Published by Fish And Other Tales, LLP

FIRST EDITION

Published by:
Fish And Other Tales, LLP
314 Booye Terrace
Northfield, New Jersey 08225
609-892-1234

Our Web Site is: www.FishAndOtherTales.com

Edited by: Christina R. Griggs

Illustrations by: Sean Johnson,
Jessie L. Higbee and David M. Jones

Cover Photo by: Gary Mirando
www.garymirando.com

TESTIMONIALS

"If you've been out at sea, it's a big place out there. It's a bit amazing these five are alive."

Brian Williams,
NJ News Correspondent

New Jersey Fishermen Tread Water in the Atlantic

Five men struggle to survive in the Atlantic Ocean after their boat sank from a huge wave crashing over the stern. Eighteen hours of treading water while hanging on to lobster pots, the men accepted death as any chance of rescue seemed to pass them by. Using flares and calling for nearby search and rescue boats just seemed to give false hope until a passing tanker heard their cries echoing in the darkness. All five men unbelievably made it out alive and, to this day, believe they were the luckiest men on earth.

One of the most amazing survival stories I have ever produced. Call it fate, call it luck, I call it the will to survive.

Tim Willison, Producer,
Outdoor Life Network
Warren Miller Entertainment

Working at an offshore fishing magazine, I am well aware of the dangers of the sea, and on a too regular basis hear stories of fishing dream trips turned into nightmares. I've read of heart attacks fifty miles from shore, fish inflicting near-fatal wounds, and the like, but few stories crossing my desk during my tenure at *Big Game Fishing Journal* have stuck with me as has David Jones's "*Escape From the Deep*" (the short story version of *Promising Forecast*). I found his ability to combine the graphic details at sea with the more psychological aspects unique among outdoor writers; it is his human aspect that makes his writing shine. He was not some adventurer/hero who tested his luck against extreme elements one too many times, but a regular guy, like me, who found a typically manageable situation transformed into the crisis of a lifetime. I, for one, would like to see more of Jones's narrative in the future.

Chris Bohlman, Managing Editor
Big Game Fishing Journal

Dedicated to

FRED PAULDING

Atlantic City's

"Monster Man"

Everyone has heard of the great Frank Mundus (also known as the "Monster Man"), the notorious shark fisherman from Montauk, New York. Quinn, the character in the movie *Jaws*, was modeled after Frank. But few have ever heard of Fred Paulding, unless you were around Captain Starn's docks during the '60's.

Fred regularly weighed sharks in over 1200 pounds. He broke the scale three times and as a result had to cut the larger sharks into two and sometimes three pieces before they would let him weigh them. The Atlantic City Press nicknamed Fred and his crew as the Paulding Posse. Fred not only loved shark fishing, but also loved sharing and teaching his skills to others.

I loved fishing with him for many reasons, one of them being his ability to make every fishing trip fun. If you made a mistake and lost a fish, there was never a cross word or ass-chewing. Instead, Fred would laugh, share a story of how he had made that same mistake, and then he would teach you what to do so you wouldn't make that mistake again. There was no pressure. We always had fun and laughs to share along with our fish stories when we got back to the docks.

Fred was invited on many tournaments and fishing trips because of his reputation and the fishing knowledge he always shared. He fished the bay, as well as the ocean, and loved to teach his sons-in-law and grandchildren everything he could about boating and fishing. He was a loving husband to his wife, Lee, and a devoted father to his two lovely daughters, Gail and Barbara. I feel blessed to have had him for a father-in-law and the grandfather of our children. Every fishing trip I go on, I think of him and try to be the kind of fisherman he was. He was greatly loved and will be missed by all that knew him. Anyone who ever fished with Fred would agree – Fred Paulding was Atlantic City's Monster Man and he will be missed.

PROLOGUE

When his body finally stopped convulsing from the cold and his vision cleared, Art gazed eastward, out across the miles of slick, glassy, black ocean toward the lights of the ships slowly gliding across the horizon. None of them were heading in their direction or even remotely looked like they might turn toward them. He was beginning to accept the fact that he was getting closer to death with every minute that passed. The shaking was more frequent and more intense. His body just couldn't produce enough heat to keep warm. It was only a matter of time before he passed out and drowned or his heart just gave out. He decided he'd do his best to stay conscious until morning. He figured the lobster boat had to check their traps sometime and was hoping to be alive when they did. He wanted his wife and son to at least have a body to bury.

Dwayne and Duffy, who were clinging to the lobster pot with him, weren't doing any better. Occasionally Art had to pull Dwayne's face out of the water when he passed out. Conversation had ceased long ago... silence reigned, and not without reason. There was no love lost between Art and these two guys, but that was a less important matter. All they wanted to do now was survive, but they could only wait and pray for a miracle. They had been in the water going on eighteen hours now.

About a mile away, clinging to another buoy, Dave and Joe were trying to keep their spirits up by sharing their life stories. It didn't keep the cold and convulsions at bay, but it did help to pass the time.

Dave wondered what had become of their shipmates after separating earlier in the day in the hopes of making their rescue more likely. He prayed Art, Duffy and Dwayne had been found and were now looking for them, but he knew deep down that any continued search wouldn't start up again until the sun came up.

He could feel his body slowly dying as time dragged on, but the worst realization was that they were all totally helpless and at the mercy of God and the elements. This helplessness was totally foreign to Dave. In the past, he had always been able to somehow make a bad situation better. Shit, he was a carpenter; he could fix anything. The irony was not lost on him as all he could do now was pray and wait.

Dave and Art, although a mile apart, had the same question on their minds... how had such a well-planned and anticipated fishing trip gone from being a wonderful life experience to a life-threatening one so quickly and without warning? Neither had an immediate answer for that question, but they both knew one simple fact – if somebody didn't find them soon, they would be dead within hours.

CHAPTER ONE

DAVE

My Uncle Ed's houseboat was nothing more than a converted cabin cruiser moored to a couple of old pilings in a small creek that led out to Lake's Bay. Abandoned years ago and left to rot, it lay with its hull deep in the mud, completely stripped of all its deck hardware, never to grace the open waters again.

During my early years of growing up, my mother would drive me, along with my brothers and sisters, down to Uncle Ed's boat which was down a small dirt road coated with crushed clam shells. The road cut right through the meadows and was full of potholes and was poorly maintained. We would drive over a small wooden bridge where there was always someone crabbing. The bridge was built of large solid timbers covered with initials and dates carved by bored crabbers over the years. At the end of the road was what the locals called Poorman's Boat Ramp. It was nothing more than a clamshell beach that would support a car and a trailer, hardly ever used with the exception of a few clammers in the spring and fall months. Between the bridge and the boat ramp was Uncle Ed's boat. There was a plank on the deck of the boat that my brothers, Vince and Ed, would have to position, which would make it possible for everyone to walk up the plank and walk down the far side of the boat to the farthest corner, which was the only corner deep enough to jump off and not get stuck in the mud.

We would swim and play all day. Just a few feet away, my mother laid in her beach chair, facing the sun with her eyes closed. Her enjoyment was expressed by the smile on her face as she listened to our sounds of play, mixed with the seagull squawks and the wind blowing over the green meadow grass.

I never saw the boat in livable condition, or for that matter met my Uncle Ed, but I had no trouble picturing him and his boat based on all the stories my mother would share with us. According to my mother, during Prohibition, my Uncle Ed was one of the best rum runners in the Atlantic City area. She based this on the fact that he knew the back bays and waterways better than anyone. Her other two supporting facts were that he had the fastest boat around and was never caught. When Prohibition ended, Uncle Ed bought the cabin cruiser and lived on it, refusing to take a regular job. He was what is known in South Jersey as a 'bay man'. A bay man is a person who spends his days making a living out of the back bays and marshlands of southern New Jersey. You can spot a bay man by his usual rough dress and carefree attitude, happy to just get by on a daily basis, not really caring what others think of him. Bay men are the envy of many people who are caught up in the rat race of everyday living.

My father liked my Uncle Ed and often credited him for saving us from starvation the winter he had his appendix taken out. Every day, Ed stopped by with no less than six ducks and a bag of potatoes. This story would always end with my dad saying that it was a wonder that we all didn't quack. My dad did not like the bay, boats or fishing; he grew up in Philadelphia and knew very little about the Jersey shore. Although he did build P.T. boats during the war, at the old boat works in West Atlantic City, he never acquired an interest in boats or water sports. Sometime after the war, a hurricane devastated the area and Uncle Ed moved away. He never contacted the family again, leaving behind the many stories and the wrecked houseboat. My mother missed him and always kept the hope of hearing from him again.

As we grew up, it was my mother who gave us free reign of the creeks and salt ponds that divided the marshland from Absecon Island. However, she laid down the law when it came to going out into the open bays and main waterways. I can truthfully say, at that point in our lives, we had no trouble obeying her rules. There was always something else to do. If the fish weren't biting, there was

crabbing and if the tide wasn't right, there was always swimming, or maybe just a good mud fight.

Boats became a big part of our growing up and added adventure to our days, in fact, it had now become impossible to have fun without one. I had three brothers and three sisters and every Christmas I would ask for a boat, but usually got crab traps or a fishing pole. I had no trouble accepting that we could not afford a boat, but never stopped hoping or asking for one at Christmas time.

Between my brothers' friends and mine, we managed to fill our needs and continued doing all the things that could be done in the bay area. There was plenty to do and lots to learn, as our goal was to become self-made bay men. We never missed a chance to make a dollar, whether it was pulling someone's boat off a mud flat after it ran aground or selling a bushel of crabs to whoever would pay us a couple of bucks. It seemed like we were always short on cash, which I might add is no excuse to steal, but we were sometimes forced to raise the skull and crossbones flag. We were liked by all the locals simply because we never got into any real trouble or hurt anyone. Our pirating would consist of stealing minnows from bait buckets to siphoning a few gallons of gas from cars or boats.

As time went on, we became more and more familiar with the back bays and were becoming accomplished boat operators. As we grew, my mother's laws and boundaries for us changed, with only one exception... and that was we were never to go near the inlet. There was danger there and we knew it. Most of my mother's fears were based on the stories that my Uncle Ed shared with her. There were many close calls for Uncle Ed and the most perilous times were coming into or leaving the inlet.

It was a well-known fact that most fishing trips were decided on the condition of the inlet. We always knew when the inlet was bad because many of the large boats would be fishing in the back bays. Whenever we were in the bait shops, almost everyone mentioned the inlet and used a different word to describe it.

We knew just about everything there was to know about the inlet from listening to the locals talk about it. We even knew where it was, but had never really seen it. The daily warnings from my mother and tales that we heard had us quite convinced that we should avoid it.

Great Egg Harbor Inlet is probably like many other inlets in the sense that it is the main channel leading out of the back bays into the ocean. One of the most common dangers that exists is that the main channel, usually marked by buoys, is constantly changing from the currents and storm tides. One side of the channel is a wall of rocks and boulders to help hold back the sea and stop erosion. The other side of the channel is a mass of water filled with unmarked sandbars and unpredictable waves. The main channel winds like a snake from the ocean into the bay. Because of the tides and wind, this area is almost always turbulent with currents and waves. Many boats have been lost coming through Great Egg Harbor Inlet and countless stories were told at the gas docks and bait shops of near mishaps while rounding the rock pile.

One summer, my brother's best friend was given a brand new Boston Whaler boat with a thirty-five horse-power Mercury outboard motor for an eighth-grade graduation present. Not only would this boat give us access to new areas, but it would help us change our image from young bay men who fish, crab or clam everyday to water skiing, fun-loving young men. I forgot to mention that we were all starting to notice girls. We were finding it almost impossible to focus on being bay men when it was now possible to water ski, swim or try to get the attention of girls. We no longer wanted to look or act like bay men and, with the acquisition of Dee's new boat, we started to change our focus.

By the end of the second summer of using Dee's boat, we felt as if we had done just about everything that you can think of doing in the bay. This was no reason for us to stop looking for or trying to have fun, though. We were still warned daily not to go near the ocean or the inlet and, although we knew the warning by heart, I never questioned my mother about it. For years, she had us convinced that there were daily shark attacks and little boys missing at sea, with their boats never seen again.

As the summer slipped by, we eventually felt compelled to further our quest for adventure. Feeling like we had already conquered the bay, it was almost like a game; each day we would get behind one of the big cabin cruisers that were headed out to sea. In the safety of their tail-wake, we felt secure. We would ride in the flat water right behind the larger boat, well within yelling range, and just follow them as they plowed a path for us through the back bays toward the forbidden inlet. As we followed our mother ship toward the treacherous waterway, we would make false promises to each other that 'this time' we would go all the way out to the ocean. Usually, the first sight of the breakers smashing against the rock pile or an unusual ground swell would be all it would take for us to turn tail and run for the protection of the bay. This game was played whenever we were bored and it would give us something to talk about until the next time. Although the fear of the unknown existed, we all knew in our hearts that before the summer would end we would conquer the inlet... and probably the ocean.

The day finally came when we would attempt to round the rock pile, knowing it meant breaking the cardinal rule our parents gave us, which only added to the adventure. We were completely mentally prepared and planned a week ahead for the big day. We had borrowed an extra gas can and topped off both tanks. Each of us had a knife, in case of shark attack, and we even had a waterproof flashlight, in case we were swept out to sea in the dark. We took all precautions to not alert our parents of our plans.

Dee, our captain, was waiting at the boat. He knew his crew well - my brother, Stan, and me. We were prepared to go down with the ship, if necessary. It was a beautiful day; the sky was blue, the sun was bright, with just a slight breeze. With conditions just right, we headed in the direction of the inlet. We picked up the first large boat that came along and grafted ourselves to his tail-wake, just like we had practiced countless times before. Captain Dee made the announcement that under no conditions would he turn back. I felt as if we were after the great white whale and had just spotted him.

You could feel the excitement building as we neared the inlet; it seemed as if the sea gulls were louder and the air had a freshness to it. Everything seemed to be going as planned and the reality of what we were doing took hold of us as we were suddenly transferred from the grassy marshland of the back bays to the white sand and waves of the inlet. The sound of the waves breaking on the rocks could be heard over the thirty-five horsepower Mercury outboard motor that never let us down - and we prayed that it wouldn't do it now.

We neared the mouth of the inlet, still following the larger boat. My brother Stan could be heard saying, "Oh God, please be with us," as the ground swells started to lift us and pull us down to where you almost had to stand up just to see land. Every wave that hit our boat would spray up and over us with a fine salty mist and would burn our eyes, which we refused to close for fear of missing the unexpected. The waves from the passing boats continuously pushed us left and right, but our captain maintained his course.

As we fought our way out, I remember looking at Dee's face; it had no sign of fear on it. However, I noticed his hands looked like those of a dead man, white and wrinkled from holding the throttle and steering wheel too tight. I was shocked even more when I looked down at my own hands that were holding the railing to see that they looked the same.

Before I could recover from that, my brother Stan yelled out, "Feel how much colder the water is here."

15

With fear in my voice, I yelled back, "Get your hand back in the boat," still thinking of my mother's stories of shark attacks.

There was not a doubt in our minds that this was the most adventurous thing we had ever done. Our journey was constant motion, noise and new sights. Turning around would be insane at this point.

Before we knew what happened, we found ourselves past the rock pile and in the open ocean for the first time in our lives. We were outside the turbulence of the inlet. Dee pulled back on the throttle as we watched the big boat we followed out pull away from us.

We stood up and looked around. We were floating on the edge of a new and exciting frontier. The bay would never again hold the excitement it once held for us. By the end of the summer, running the rock pile became routine. As the summers passed and the years went by, our lives changed. However, I never lost my love for the back bays or the ocean. I consider myself a self-made 'bay man'. Even though I do not dress or act like one, in my heart, I know I could be one.

CHAPTER TWO

I had just turned seventeen and started driving. My older brother, Vince, invited me to go striper fishing and all I had to do was pick up some live eels for bait and meet him at his house in Margate. When I pulled up in front of his house, I saw Vince putting his fishing poles into the thirteen-foot Boston Whaler, which was on a trailer in his driveway.

I was walking over to meet him, holding the five-gallon bucket of eels, when the door to the house opened and out walked the greatest distraction I had ever seen in my life. I turned my head to look at her, but never stopped walking and, as I took in the sight of what I thought was the most beautiful thing I had ever seen, I walked right into the front of my brother's boat, knocking the bucket of eels into the air. Half of the eels spilled into the boat and half of them onto the ground.

Most of the water spilled on me as I heard my brother yell, "What the hell are you doing, you simple ass?"

I stopped looking at the girl and was suddenly confronted with what was going on around me. About six of the eels that had fallen into the boat were squirming around looking for hiding places, while my brother was starting to pick up the fishing poles and bags of gear he had just put into the boat. I looked down at my feet to see the other six eels squirming in different directions on the ground. I bent down and started grabbing at them, trying to pick them up and put them back into the bucket. I got all of them off the ground but, as I started to stand up, I hit my head on the boat and almost dropped the bucket again.

Vince yelled out, "Barbara, would you please go back into the house before he kills one of us?" Vince has always been a protective and very loving brother. I would say he was the perfect big brother.

"Are you okay?" the beautiful girl asked me.

Still trying to recover from the mess and not being in the right frame of mind, I smiled and said, "I'm a carpenter." She smiled at me and went back into the house. All I could think about was what the hell I had just said... "I'm a carpenter".

I turned around to face my brother, who was now laughing out loud. "Oh, Mister Carpenter. Would you mind giving me a hand with these eels you spilled into my boat?"

The eels were finally in the bucket and we were set to leave when Vince said, "If you promise not to move, I'll introduce you to our babysitter."

Vince turned and, in a much more pleasant voice, asked Barbara to come out again. I thought I had regained my composure but, the minute she stepped out of the house, I felt myself worrying about what to say next. I had never had a girl have an effect on me like this in my life.

Forgetting about the eel slime and water I had all over me, I put out my hand only to have her look at it and say, "Maybe next time." She started to laugh, then said, "You're a mess." It hadn't dawned on me until I looked down at myself. I really felt like I had made a fool of myself in front of her.

For the first time in my life, I couldn't wait for a fishing trip to end so I could get back to see her. When we returned, my brother not only reintroduced me to Barbara, but let me drive her home in his new car, a red Mustang with a white convertible top, which he never let anyone else drive.

As it turned out, Barbara's father, Fred Paulding, was a nail gun salesman. Within a week, he was at one of my Dad's construction sites to try to sell us a nail gun system. During the sales pitch, the subject of fishing came up and, as part of the nail gun purchase, I got invited on a shark fishing trip with Fred.

I have always been proud of my knowledge of the back bays and my fishing experience and I never had trouble talking about fishing or boating, except when I spoke to people who went deep-sea fishing. I just couldn't understand their total lack of interest in the back bays and inlets, where I was quite content with my fishing and boating skills. I had never been asked to go deep-sea fishing or, for that matter, knew anyone that fished the ocean well enough who would be interested in teaching me – that is until I met Fred.

Fred and I hit it off from day one; not only was he knowledgeable about deep-sea fishing, but he also enjoyed teaching and sharing his fishing knowledge with me. At that time, Fred was considered by *The Atlantic City Press* to be one of the best shark fishermen around. *The Press* even gave Fred and his crew a nickname – 'The Paulding Posse'. Fred was so successful at shark fishing that, whenever he brought his catch in to get weighed at Captain Starn's in Atlantic City, the dock master would make him cut the bigger fish in two because he had broken their scale three times in the past with sharks weighing over twelve hundred pounds.

Fred was not only one of the most experienced fishermen I have ever known, but he was also lots of fun to fish with. Every fishing trip became a learning experience. After three years of fishing with Fred, my confidence was tempered. Ocean fishing and big game fishing was what I wanted to do. This used to drive my poor father nuts. At that time, he really did depend on me in the family building business.

By the time I was thirty-six, my father had been retired for four years and I had total responsibility for our family building business. It took most of my time and it was almost impossible to plan a trip. In fact, the only time I ever got to go deep-sea fishing was when I got a spur-of-the-moment invitation and, if the fish weren't biting, I usually turned it down. I really picked my trips now and enjoyed them more than ever. If the trip didn't have the few basic conditions needed to ensure success, I would make the decision to work or spend the time with my family, which at this time consisted of three beautiful little girls Lisa, Laura and Lynn, and my lovely wife, Barbara.

I tried to fish as much as possible without affecting family and work. It seemed like all I ever did was work to keep the business going. I remember sharing this thought with my wife, who would snap me back to reality by asking if I would prefer to do the laundry and cooking. Although sympathy was hard to get, I always got her understanding when it came time for a fishing trip. My wife knows I love to fish and always puts up with my sickness (addiction). We had been married fifteen years and knew each other's needs.

🐋 🐋 🐋 🐋 🐋 🐋

The fishing season was at its peak and my father-in-law, who had really slowed down but had not stopped his fishing, called with some exciting news. He had a client who had invited him and his two sons-in-law on a giant tuna fishing trip out of Montauk, New York. I was so excited I couldn't stand it. Not only would this be a once-in-a-lifetime experience, but it would also give me a chance to see how they fished for tuna in New York.

I couldn't understand why my wife wasn't overcome with joy for me. The fact that Bill, my brother-in-law, couldn't make it helped to fuel her discontent. Bill, Fred and I had gone on almost every major fishing trip together in the past. Barb always felt better knowing that we had each other's backs. After using every excuse in the book on Barb as to why I should still go fishing, I had to resort to calling on my father-in-law to soften her up, and Fred, as everybody knew, had the ability to change anybody's mind about anything. The trip was a couple of weeks off and I knew I could win her over before the reservation deadline. There were plenty of reasons why I shouldn't go and a few good ones why I should. I had three big jobs started, I didn't have any extra cash and it seemed like a long time since I had taken the kids anywhere. On the other hand, I would gain a lot of fishing knowledge and there was always the chance of catching enough fish to pay our expenses... and it was only a four-day excursion. I had totally convinced myself that I had to go, so I decided to be selfish and told Fred to sign me up.

At the time, this trip seemed like the most important happening in my life. This, I might add, was the only time I ever saw my wife upset about me going fishing. I could not concentrate on a single thing but the upcoming adventure. All I could think about was reeling in a giant tuna or, better yet, an eight hundred pound mako. Time would not pass fast enough for me. I would be at work all day and not remember half of the day's events for thinking about catching tuna. I found myself useless in just about all phases of my life. All I wanted to do was go to Montauk and fish. I should have taken off the two weeks before the trip because I couldn't do anything but think about it. This really angered my wife, who knew all along what was going on in my head. I just kept thinking that she was going to be happier when we were home again.

My wife enjoys bay fishing and crabbing, even a day on the mud flats clamming, but when it comes to fishing in the ocean, it's a dead no-no. 'I don't care how good they are biting,' was always her reply. My wife always gets seasick and never has enjoyed being in the ocean. Even a cruise that we took on our thirteenth wedding anniversary was a nightmare due to her seasickness. Once, though, I talked her into renting a houseboat in the Chesapeake Bay. This turned out to be a one-time pleasant experience.

I'm not sure a person knows when he or she has become addicted and it might sound silly that I compare my love of fishing and boating to such an addiction, but I am. So, when it comes to getting Barb's blessing so I can go, I will never stop trying.

Much to my disbelief, the day finally arrived. By this time, my wife couldn't wait for me to go and get this fishing trip out of my system and, as the kids lined up for their good-bye kisses and with Barb at the end of the line, I promised the girls presents for all when

I returned. As I kissed Barb good-bye, she hugged me and whispered in my ear, "I love you. Have a good time."

It was from that minute on that I relaxed. It really meant a lot for me to go with her blessing. I had made everyone in the house and on the job a nervous wreck over the last two weeks and just hearing her say to be careful and to have a good time was all that was needed.

Montauk was one of the best trips I think I ever had. Fred and I had such a good time, even though, because of the weather, we only got to go fishing one day. Amazingly, we still managed to catch enough tuna to pay for all of the expenses.

When I got home, I got a hero's welcome from my family, along with headaches and problems that developed in my absence from the business. But, after a good night's sleep, I felt I could handle anything.

It was the last part of August and our fishing season was still going strong, but nearing its end. I had contracted to build a house for an old friend I had gone to school with. When I returned to the site, there was a message that Jeff had been trying to get in touch with me. At the time, this was one of my biggest jobs and I gave it top billing on my list of priorities.

When I met with my friend, Jeff, he explained to me that he had a contractor he wanted me to use on his house. At first thought, I was ready to argue. Jeff, a well-established real estate agent, was prepared for that and, before I could get a word out of my mouth, he said, "Could you do me a favor just this once? I'll take all responsibility for his work because I'm recommending him."

I had been in the contracting business long enough to know that whenever you can avoid an argument, do it.

A good businessman, Jeff was ready, almost as if he had rehearsed. He began explaining about the new high-efficiency heating system he wanted installed in his house and how his contractor was the only one in the area who was certified to install it. It was a good reason and I had not contracted the heat out yet (due to my preparation for the Montauk fishing trip).

"My guys are good and I like them and they like me."

"I know, and that's why I'm asking you, as a favor. I promise not to interfere in any more of the job."

I was expecting more problems than this and, if we could keep this job simple, I was going to do everything I could.

"If you say he's good, that's fine with me. I would like to meet him and go over the plans."

"Great! I really want to thank you for this. I think you and Duffy are going to get along well. He's a fisherman, too."

Jeff took care of setting up a time when I could meet Duffy and go over the plans. I'm a general contractor and I'm very loyal to my subcontractors. They treat me well and I treat them well and, after awhile, we built a trust in each other. I was meeting with a new subcontractor, or so I thought. It turned out that the fellow I was going to see was a very successful businessman and needed my work like he needed a hole in his head. When I stopped by his office, I was impressed from the minute I walked in. After giving my name to the secretary, I had about two minutes to check out his shop, which was quite busy with employees. He had a sizable operation going on.

The secretary called to me and said, "Go right up. Duffy is expecting you."

With blueprints in hand, I started up the stairway, already preparing myself for what would normally go on in a meeting like this. Once in his office, a well-dressed guy came over and introduced himself. I was used to a lot of different situations and was very rarely intimidated. For some reason, I felt Duffy would have felt more comfortable if I was. Anyway, with the introduction over, I got right to the business of Jeff's house. I immediately realized that it didn't mean much to Duffy, as he would only give it to one of his foremen.

Duffy's office was decorated with pictures of all kinds. I kept looking for a connection between him and Jeff and when I couldn't find one, I asked. Duffy's reply was that he knew Jeff's boss really well. So that answered my question.

"Jeff tells me you're a fisherman."

"Yes, I'm getting into it big-time right now."

"What kind of boat do you have?"

This was the wrong question to ask, because I couldn't stop him from talking about it. Duffy handed me a picture of the boat. While I was looking at the picture, he started stating all the facts about the boat.

"It's a thirty-two-foot Scorpion made by Chris Craft with twin, two-hundred-horsepower, Mercury outboards. She'll do fifty-five miles an hour in five-foot seas. Next week I'm having two new propellers put on, which will take it up to sixty-five."

It was easy to see that Duffy had the same 'sickness' about boats and fishing as I did. His boat looked beautiful in the picture. It had sleek lines and a black hull with the name of the boat written down the side of it – 'Hot Stuff'.

"Who named the boat?" I asked.

"I did, after my first ride in it."

I realized we'd been in his office about two hours talking about his boat. So, I started to fill him in on my fishing experiences. He started asking questions like, "So you fish the canyons a lot?"

I no sooner got done telling him about my Montauk trip when he invited me to go fishing next week. "What are you going for?" I asked.

All of a sudden, I noticed he had lowered his voice. He confessed that he knew very little about fishing and was trying to learn anything he could. I openly volunteered to help in whatever way I could. I ended our meeting by confirming a day to go fishing with him. For some reason, I was in a good mood the rest of the day. I kept laughing to myself about whether Jeff knew what he had done for me.

That night, when I got home, my wife was in the kitchen cooking. I came up behind her, grabbed her and kissed her neck.

"So, how was your day, dear?" she said.

Feeling something was up, I said, "Okay, why?"

"Oh, I thought you'd like to know that 'Duffy's' secretary called and wanted to confirm Wednesday as the fishing trip, if that's okay with you."

"Wow! This guy really wants to go fishing," I said.

"What do you mean? You just got back from three days of fishing last night and you're planning another trip next week? Oh, and before I forget, she said, 'Please bring a friend'."

"Art."

"What?"

"Art. I'll invite Art."

"You better check with Art. I don't know if he's as rich as you and I."

"Honey, we'll be alright. I promise you. This is business and I think it will work out for the better."

I remember being a little upset over the fact that I didn't get the chance to tell my wife myself about going fishing the next week. But, in a way, it made it a little easier to not have to explain why I should take another working day off for fishing. Just to be on the safe side, I put in a word of defense, "Look, aside from the Montauk trip, I've done hardly any fishing at all, except for a few 'tog trips with Art in the spring. ('Tog is the local term for tautog, also known as blackfish). Besides, this guy Duffy is a big contractor. I might get some really big work from him."

"Just remember, I'm here answering the phone all day. What should I tell everyone?"

"I promise I'll take care of everything."

After dinner was over, I felt my fishing sickness coming on. So, I went into my office, picked up *The Press* and thumbed through until I found the fishing report. What I read was exactly what I had expected – nothing great, but not bad either. I already knew we would be fishing the Twenty-eight Mile Wreck, where the report stated small yellow-fin, tuna, dolphin and slammer blues were being caught, but not in great numbers.

Pulling out a chart of the Wreck, I started putting together a probable course, which included traveling South to a few spots where the bottom is uneven and drops in different areas. If Duffy's boat is as fast as he said it is, there would be no trouble fishing these areas in the course of a day.

Next on the list – call Art. I already knew he'd go because of trips in the past. Art could go on any trip if he had a three-day notice, which is what he needed to reschedule his patients in his chiropractic office. We both used the same rule for big trips and for small trips – just a phone call. As I dialed the number, I said to myself, "Yellow-fin and dolphin."

"Hello, Anna? It's Dave. Is Art around?"

"He's got office hours tonight, but you can call him."

Before I could thank her and say good-bye, she asked, "Have you been fishing?" I told her about my Montauk trip.

"Please take Art fishing, will you? He needs a break."

This was music to my ears. My sickness was getting worse. I called Art, who answered the phone on the second ring, "Hello, Dr. Higbee."

"Yellow-fin and dolphin," was all I said. This was how Art and I would always start a conversation if it ended in a fishing trip invitation.

"Dave! When?"

I could tell Art's sickness was just beginning. "Next Wednesday. Just bring your lunch. I'll call you back with all the details tomorrow. Are you in?"

"Yup!"

"See you Wednesday."

ART

I was really excited after hanging up from Dave's call. I hadn't been on an offshore trip for quite a while and was Jonesin' for some fresh tuna. I was lucky to have Dave as a friend who would think to call me when these opportunities came up.

Dave and I go way back. We went to grade school and high school together, but actually became fishing buddies after I finished college. We ran into each other down at Hackney's Boatyard. Dave had recently purchased a twenty-five foot, wooden Lapstrake inboard named the *Quahog* and was docking it at Hackney's where I was working at the time with my friend/roommate, Dan. Dan and I had also recently purchased a thirty-foot Holtz wooden boat and were docking it at Hackney's, too. People who own wooden boats immediately form a bond because there is no bigger pain in the ass than trying to maintain them. It's constant work and maintenance, so any tips or tricks to make it easier are eagerly sought after and shared.

At the time, fiberglass hulls had pretty much taken over the industry, but there were still holdouts and a lot of them were at Hackney's. There is something innately beautiful about a well-built and designed wooden boat. Troth, Pacemaker, Viking, Holtz, Yank and Egg Harbor were some of the local boat builders whose hulls still graced Hackney's. Unfortunately, over the years, they have all but disappeared, having fallen into disrepair and relegated to the scrap heap.

My buddy Dan and I grew up together, he being the brother I never had. I owe a large thanks to him for my interest in boating and fishing. When we were twelve years old, his father, 'Big Ed', found a two-man duck boat and powered it with a five-horse, Sears, air-cooled outboard and a set of oars - just in case. For the next few years, we traveled the back bays between the mainland and Absecon Island fishing, clamming and crabbing. Our parents turned us loose in the morning and picked us up in the afternoon. We discovered a whole new world out there in the salt marsh.

I didn't understand how most people who drove over the causeway, traversing the meadows, thought of it as a wasteland or just so much mud, grass and water to be crossed over. To us, it was a multifaceted world where every trip brought new learning experiences and respect for Mother Nature and all her creatures. Not to mention the adventures and the fun that could be had by two kids turned loose in a very large playground. As we got older, activities extended to waterfowl hunting, commercial clamming and waterskiing. As long as it was out in the bay, it was good.

It came as no surprise that Dan and I wound up becoming the proud owners of a recently refurbished thirty-foot, diesel powered, wooden hulled Holtz. It was a beautiful boat, originally commissioned for the Army Corps of Engineers to survey the Delaware Bay. It had a uniquely designed hull with a box keel and two portholes built into the bottom to look through; I'm still trying to figure that one out, since Delaware Bay is not known for the water's visual clarity. At any rate, the hull was found washed up and abandoned on Brigantine Beach by one of the Holtz family, who then decided to haul it back to Holtz Boatworks in Tuckahoe and completely refurbish and repower her.

Danny came home one day really excited about this boat. A mutual friend of the Holtz family had informed him it was for sale for a mere five thousand dollars. It might as well have been five hundred thousand to us. We were making twenty dollars a day at the boatyard and had enough trouble paying the electric bill, let alone having enough money to buy a boat. So, even though we were basically broke, we went to look at this boat and immediately fell in love with it.

A white pilot house had been added forward, along with a forward deck and trim made out of varnished mahogany. The hull was tugboat style with a high prow and painted glossy black. The back two-thirds of the boat was wide open for fishing or whatever else came to mind. It had been repowered with a new GM Bedford, six-cylinder diesel and outfitted with a Loran navigation system, depth-finder and huge, through-the-roof search light. There was not another boat like it anywhere on the East coast. So, of course, being two young, single and extremely poor guys, we just had to figure out a way to buy this boat. An opportunity like this only comes around once, so we scrounged, begged and borrowed and somehow came up with the cash. We were now the proud owners of an original. Now if we could only afford to fill the fuel tanks.

Danny had some experience with boats in the thirty-foot class. His dad (Big Ed, of the two-man, duck boat fame) owned a twenty-eight foot Cruisealong that he used to take us out in as kids and Dan had owned a thirty-foot Pacemaker, flying bridge and all. This boat is the one he and I learned to shoot the rock pile in to get through the Great Egg Harbor Inlet. Ask any local captain about shootin' the rock pile and they'll know exactly what you're talking about. It's the quickest way to get through the inlet to deep water, but can sometimes be very rough. The general rule is - if you can't get out at the

rock pile... don't go out, a rule we followed for many years.

By the way, Dan had named his boat *Agatha*, after his late mom. He was a good man.

The two years I spent working at Hackney's Boatyard were two of the most fun and interesting years of my life, up until that point anyway. I learned more about fixing, hauling, storing, piloting and blocking boats than in all the years before or since. Corky Hackney was a patient man. He had to be; he hired me, thanks to Dan. At that time, I didn't know jack shit about boats or fixing anything. But I was willing to learn.

Unfortunately, some of that learning was at Corky's expense. That would explain why we were only making twenty dollars a day. But the benefits were good. Lunch and, most times, dinner at the Tilton Inn were on Corky. Did I mention lunch and dinner included recreational beverages? Our Christmas bonus that year was twenty-five pounds of king crab legs. Besides all the shits and giggles, what more could two young single guys ask for?

🐋 🐋 🐋 🐋 🐋 🐋

One day, while Dan was at the other end of the yard tuning up somebody's boat, Corky asked me to come with him to move a boat on a trailer. I jumped into the cab of his old International and we crossed the yard to where a forty-two foot Viking was sitting on one of Corky's two homemade trailers. I'm talking welded steel beam, heavy-duty trailer with three axles and six tires and a twenty-foot tongue that he used to pull the bigger boats out of the water. It was the dead of winter, two of the tires were flat and all the tires were sitting in a low, soft spot. It didn't look good to me, but what did I know?

So, Corky pulls the International, front first, up to the trailer (the hitch is on the front of the truck) and says to me, "Go get the trailer tongue on the hitch plate and put the pin in."

Acting like I know what I'm doing, I say, "Okay, Corky, the pin is in." And it was, but not quite in the right place. Are you beginning to see what might happen here? He starts rocking the trailer back and forth, harder and harder each time, until finally the safety pin pops out and the twenty-foot long trailer tongue spears the grill, radiator and the hood of his beloved truck.

With steam pouring out of the truck, and Corky's ears, he stepped down off the running board and walked to the front of the truck to view the carnage. It wasn't pretty. The yard truck was now officially out of commission. Danny came running over from the other side of the yard after hearing the impact, yelling, "What the hell happened?" I had no clue, so I kept my mouth shut.

Corky looked right at me and asked, "Are you sure you put the pin in?"

"Yup," I said.

"Show me where you put the trailer tongue."

I did and he just rolled his eyes and walked away. Apparently, it wasn't the right place and I figured my career in the boatyard was over.

Danny said to me, "Don't worry. He'll calm down. Besides, he can't afford to fire you; we work too cheap." With that, we busted up laughing.

About an hour later, Corky came back and said to me, "Well, you broke it so you're gonna have to fix it."

Dan and I spent the next three days in exile at Fleming's Junk Yard out in Egg Harbor Township scouring the yard for International parts. That was an education in itself. We found the parts and fixed the truck and all was well, at least for then.

Once I had broken the ice with that bonehead maneuver, I always asked exactly what I was supposed to do, and how, if I wasn't sure. Gradually my confidence grew and, before long, I could handle most of the tasks required of me. Corky started talking to me again and life was good.

Dan and I decided to name our boat the "*Sealapper*". It was a great bay boat and large enough to be ocean-going, but only under certain conditions. Because it was a round chined hull, with no deep V, and a shallow keel, it would rock and roll in a small sea and be down-right uncomfortable. So, we were limited as to how far out we could go and extremely dependent on weather forecasts.

Even with these limitations, we were able to experience a number of offshore trips, usually inside the Twenty-eight Mile Wreck. Most of these trips were shark trips, but we fished for whatever was running – from blues, flounder and weakies to striper and sharks. We also spent many a night camping out on the boat and even crabbing off the back of it while in the dock.

Between docking the boat and maintaining it and working at the boatyard, we practically lived there. It was a kind of love-hate relationship; we loved being around the bay and boats, but hated the dirty work and low pay.

One of the fringe benefits of working weekends at the yard was the entertainment factor. During the summer especially, because a lot of shoobies would come down to use their boats and a fair percentage of them didn't know what the hell they were doing. This would result in a high rate and quality of entertainment for those of us who were regulars or worked there. The center of entertainment was usually in the immediate vicinity of the boat ramp and all eyes would automatically turn in that direction when the words, "It's showtime," were spoken.

'Shoobie' is a term used in South Jersey to describe daytrippers, a tourist here for the day, mostly to go to the beach during the summer. The term became popular in the 1920s, '30s and '40s and derived from the habit of some daytrippers of bringing their lunches in shoeboxes, thus depriving the local merchants of revenue the tourists would have spent on food. Over the years, the term has expanded to include anyone from out-of-town that was down to the shore for the day or weekend.

If you have ever tried to back up a vehicle with a trailer attached, you know there is a learning curve involved with developing that skill. Watching somebody take twenty minutes to do something that should take two is kind of like watching grass grow, so we would liven things up with friendly wagers. "I'll bet you a beer it's gonna take this guy at least three tries to get that boat down the ramp," Dan would say. "Shit, I'll bet you lunch it takes him five," was my typical reply. Since Corky was usually buying anyway, we couldn't lose.

More fun than watching boats go in was watching people trying to dock them after a long day of fishing and drinking, especially when the tide and wind were ripping. It could be downright hysterical, kind of a nautical version of the Benny Hill Show. Sunday afternoons were prime time.

The goal of every captain is to get his boat into the dock smoothly and cleanly on the first attempt, without banging into pilings or other boats. But it's not like driving a car; there are no brakes and the wind and currents will eat you up if you ignore them and don't use them to your advantage. If you have a single-screw boat, it's even more difficult. Throw in the effects of alcohol and you definitely have comedy in the making. We watched many a captain bounce his boat off every piling in sight, sometimes causing damage to his boat or to others... creating more work for us. Occasionally, they would give up after numerous attempts and use a boat hook to dock the boat manually. That was the ultimate embarrassment.

There were a few that would wind up at the end of the creek, stuck in the mud because they couldn't turn their vessel around due to a ripping tide and wind. We would then have to get the workboat and tow them to their dock. How humiliating is that?

But the most hysterical events were usually performed by the shoobie know-it-alls who seemed to always be in a hurry and were obnoxious and rude. Like the guy who couldn't wait his turn to use the ramp, cut in front of someone and proceeded to back his boat down the ramp at a high rate of speed and slammed on the brakes so he wouldn't have to push his boat off, forgetting he had removed the winch cable and had no other rope attached to his boat. 'Thar she goes!' Nobody would help him retrieve his boat.

Then there was the poor guy who, when winching his boat out of the water, forgot to put his truck in gear and his emergency brake on. We pulled more than one vehicle out of the drink because of that oversight. So there was always entertainment to be had and,

of course, no one wanted to be the entertainer. Boatyard humor...
you had to be there to fully appreciate it.

In addition to ocean fishing trips, Dave and I would
occasionally fish for 'tog when they were running. Fishing for 'tog is
an art form with a definite learning curve. 'Tog, also known as
blackfish, tautog and slippery bass, are notorious bait stealers. There
can be days when it takes ten to fifteen pieces of bait to hook one
fish. They can suck the meat of a crab right out of the shell and leave
it hanging on your hook and you might not even know they've been
there. Consequently, you have to be sure to have plenty of bait or
you won't be fishing for long.

The most effective bait is calico crabs; they're easy to catch,
plentiful and they are like candy to 'tog. We would spend thirty to
forty-five minutes catching them to fill a five-gallon spackle bucket,
plenty for a decent haul of 'tog. Then we'd go tie up to the old
Ocean City-Longport Bridge and start fishing. 'Tog love structures
like rocks, pilings and even sod banks. They eat crabs, clams, mussels
and sand fleas. When they're running, the action is fast and furious.
Thirty to sixty fish per trip was common. One trip, my wife's Uncle
Frank and I topped out at one hundred and ten 'tog. All were at
least three pounds and up to twelve. Of course, that was before the
days of limits.

For years, 'tog was considered trash fish. That's when the
fishing was best because nobody, except the few in-the-know, wanted
them. They are not the most attractive looking fish, sporting thick
rubbery lips and conical-shaped buck teeth. And they are nicknamed
slippery bass for a reason. When word got out what great fighters
they were and how tasty they fried up, it was downhill from there.

We would pull up to our favorite spot and, invariably, there
were boats in the area fishing for other species like weakies, flounder
and striper. Within five minutes, we'd be pulling in fish after fish,

five to eight pounds apiece, and that always got people's attention. They would literally pull up within twenty feet to see and ask us what kind of fish they were and what kind of bait we were using. We would give them just enough info to make them happy, but not enough to make them successful. At least not without doing their homework. Fishermen don't just give away their secret spots and techniques to strangers for no reason.

Dave and I have had numerous successful fishing trips together, so when he called me to invite me to the Twenty-eight Mile Wreck, I was ready to go. When he described the boat we would be going on, I was even more intrigued. I had never been a fan of "go-fast" boats and, in fact, downright despised them. Especially when operated by shoobies, who generally had no regard for boating etiquette or safety.

I had almost been run over and swamped by one of those idiots while bay fishing in my fourteen-foot runabout. I was drifting for flounder in Risley's Channel when this clown came around the bend doing sixty miles an hour, coming within fifteen feet of me. I'm not a fan of having boats going that fast coming that close to me. It's no good for my heart. And do you think this guy slowed down after the near miss? ... Of course not. I watched him weave his way through another dozen drifting fishing boats on his way out to the Great Egg Inlet. Not once did he look back to see if his wake had swamped anybody. He couldn't have cared less.

Most "go-fast" boats that were inboards were also obnoxiously loud. If they were within a mile of you, you couldn't have a conversation with the person next to you until they passed by. They were built for one reason only, and that was speed. You couldn't exactly fish for flounder out of them. So, when Dave started to describe Duffy's boat to me, I was at first a little concerned.

When I learned that Duffy's boat was a center-console and that it was designed for fishing, I started to feel a little more comfortable about it. Finding out that it was powered by two outboards made me feel even better. Then, when Dave explained how much more fishing time we would have, I caved in and put aside my angst about "go-fast" boats ... at least this one. Now, I was totally jacked up for this fishing trip and I was just waiting for Dave's final confirmation for next Wednesday.

DAVE

The next day, I called Duffy at the shop. I started to become friendly with Duffy's secretary, who said, "You're the only one he'll call back."

"Why's that?" I asked.

"Because you're the guy who knows about fishing, aren't you?"

"All I know is I like it."

"Well, do me a favor and catch some fish. They never catch anything."

"Maybe that'll change. We're going out Wednesday."

"Really?" she laughed. "That's all we have heard about since yesterday."

I laughed and said, "It's a sickness."

"Anyway, Duffy won't be in all day, but he wants you to call him at home tonight. He also asked if you would mind not giving his home phone number to anyone."

"No problem."

That night, I called Duffy. He answered the phone and immediately bombarded me with questions pertaining to the up-coming fishing trip. I told him I had everything we needed, but he insisted on buying all the same equipment so he would have it for the future. I answered all of his questions and added quite a few items to the list he was preparing.

As the week slowly went by, I grew impatient for the day of the trip, reading the fishing reports and asking anyone I thought would know if they were catching anything and where. I prepared all my gear, just in case Duffy missed anything and, when Tuesday came, I called Duffy's office to go over the plans, only to get Linda, Duffy's secretary.

"Oh, Dave, Duffy wants you to call him at home tonight to go over things. He's out finishing up getting what he needs for the trip. What are you guys going for, anyway? I've never seen him so excited."

"Hopefully, yellow fin and dolphin at the Twenty-eight Mile Wreck."

"Wow! Does he know that?"

"I think so, why?"

"I don't think he's ever been out that far. He's only had the boat for six weeks."

"Well, he's got a good crew and I already checked the weather. It's supposed to be perfect."

"I know – he's had me check it every day."

After I hung up the phone, I started to get a little better picture of just what kind of fisherman Duffy was.

Art had been calling me every night for a week asking me if we were still on for Wednesday. "You bet!" was the standard answer.

I was daydreaming about finding a school of feeding tuna and filling the boat with them, having all four poles screaming out line at the same time. Wouldn't that be a neat first-time deep-sea fishing trip for Duffy, I thought. I really do like the fun and excitement of big game fishing.

When I returned home, there was a message on my desk, which simply said, "Call your fishing buddy."

Without a thought, I called Art, who answered, "No, I didn't call, but I was going to."

"Must be Duffy – I'll call you after I get all the information."

Next call was to Duffy, who seemed like he was in a really good mood. "What marina do you dock at, Duffy?"

"Oh, I keep the boat right behind my house here."

Duffy liked to surprise me with his lifestyle and, believe me, it wasn't hard to do.

CHAPTER THREE

DAVE

I had no trouble getting up early Wednesday morning. I had delegated the work I needed to be done to the guys that worked for me, loaded the truck and was on my way to pick up Art.

Art and I pretty much grew up together. By that, I mean we went to school together and were always friends, but never really hung out together. We renewed our friendship at Hackney's Boat Yard on the Margate Boulevard. Art worked for Wayne 'Corky' Hackney for two years while he was going to school to become a chiropractor. We both had boats there and have been good fishing buddies ever since. Art was never mean to anybody and I can honestly say I don't think there's a bad bone in his body. He's always a good friend.

Art was standing in his driveway behind a couple of plastic bags and a small cooler. Both of us were glad to be going and decided we were going to spend the rest of the day enjoying this fishing trip. Duffy gave me good directions on how to get to his house the night before and, within twenty minutes, we were parked and trying to figure out the best way to get our gear down to the boat.

There wasn't a cloud in the sky and the sun was almost blinding as we got out of the truck in front of Duffy's house. We heard the sound of Duffy's voice, yelling, "Hold on, I'll be right out." Duffy appeared from a door at the corner of the house and told us, "Just go down the hall and out the back door. You'll see the boat."

Duffy's house was located right on the inland waterway in a very rich neighborhood. It was hard not to be overwhelmed with everything that was around us, from houses to cars and boats. They were completely out of our league. As a joke, Art said, "Hey, Dave... I don't think we're in Kansas anymore". When I opened the door at the end of the hall, I turned to Art and said, "We're not at Hackney's either." Both of us laughed as we exited the hallway and found ourselves on the deck of a really nice dock that led out to the boat.

The pictures I had seen in Duffy's office were nothing compared to seeing the actual boat. It was even more impressive than I thought it would be. It looked like it was as long as the dock.

As we got closer, it was easy to see that not a nickel was spared on outfitting it. This type of boat was not known for its fishing ability, but there was a new wave of interest in outfitting them for offshore fishing because of their great speed. The boat was thirty-two feet long and only eight feet wide at its widest point. On the back, raised up out of the water, were two, two-hundred horsepower motors.

Art and I were both feeling good about this trip as we set some of our gear down on the deck and headed back to the truck for the rest of it.

When we returned to the boat, Duffy was on-deck and introduced us to his friend, Dwayne, who said, "Hi, how you guys doing?" then added, "What are you doing with all that stuff?"

"Most of this stuff is needed and some of it I like to have - just in case," I said.

When Dwayne continued and asked, "What are you going to do with those," referring to the two light poles I had in my hand, I started looking for Duffy so I could ask him who this guy thought he was, but I noticed that Duffy was trying to avoid this whole conversation by kneeling down in front of the boat, putting some things away and getting some charts out.

I turned my head back to Dwayne and answered, "If we run into a school of blues, I plan on casting into them. Why? Do you have some on board already?"

"No. And I don't think we need them either."

With that said, I stepped into the boat, looked Dwayne right in the eye and said, "Don't worry. I'll make sure they don't get in your way."

As I walked toward the bow of the boat, I turned around and looked at Art, who was just a few steps behind me. I said to Art in a low voice, "Friendly guy, huh?"

Art's reply was. "Oh, really? I think he's a jackass."

We both had a chuckle and started to store our gear for the trip. As we moved forward, I confronted Duffy, who was looking more serious than I had ever seen him look.

"Everything all right?" I asked.

"Yeah, I'm just trying not to forget anything before we get under way."

"What do you want us to do?" Art asked.

"Nothing. We're good. We'll be getting under way soon," Duffy said.

In less than a minute, we had our gear put away and started to wander around the boat, checking things out and wondering what was next.

Both Art and I had jeans and tee shirts on. We looked silly next to Duffy and Dwayne, who each had on nice windbreakers and matching pants. Every time I asked if there was something we could do, we were told, "No, we got it."

It was now ten-thirty and getting pretty hot just sitting at the dock. This trip was starting to lose its glow when we finally heard the engine beepers go off, which meant the engines were being lowered into the water. With any luck, we'd be pulling out soon.

I couldn't believe Duffy's change in attitude. He really was uptight: maybe it was all the prep work for the trip; maybe it was giving up some of his command to Dwayne's self-proclaimed expertise; or perhaps it was due to the fact Duffy had not had that much fishing experience. My only hope was that he would loosen up if we started catching some fish.

Art and I both jumped at the opportunity to do something as we pulled out. We walked the length of the boat, keeping it from bumping any of the pilings. Once we were free of the dock, our spirits rose – we were finally getting under way.

Without ever having to go fast, we were at the inlet. Even though it was a weekday, there seemed to be plenty of boats on the water and both Art and I were waiting to see what this baby would do. Boy, were we surprised.

Dwayne left the center console and started rigging poles.

"What are you doing?" I asked Dwayne.

"We're going to troll for awhile."

"Need a hand?" I asked.

"No."

With this information in hand, I went to Duffy, who was at the wheel and heading for the three-mile buoy.

"Aren't we going to the Wreck?" I asked.

"Yeah, but we're going to troll out a ways first."

It was then that I began to regret taking the day off. I went up front and sat down across from Art. He looked at me, gave me a dumb look, then put his hands out the same way you would to show someone you were out of money or puzzled.

After about an hour and a half of just trolling, I grabbed my lunch and started eating. I asked Art how he was doing.

"I'm just totally relaxed," he said, enjoying being away from it all.

It was still hard to talk to Dwayne for some reason. He just didn't want to be friendly.

Art said, "Boy, I sure would like to hear one of the poles light up."

I said, "Yeah, me too, but I really don't think that's going to happen until we get into some deeper water."

I yelled back to Duffy, "Do you guys want a soda?"

Duffy left his position and came forward. "What do you think we should do?"

"What do I think?" I was starting to feel a little moody. "Let's pick up and run for a half hour or so. You're wasting all this good fishing time trolling and you haven't even seen a bird in the last half hour."

Upon hearing this, Duffy agreed and returned to the center console, where Dwayne was searching the horizon for bird play. Duffy signaled for help to start pulling the lines in. It was the first chance Art and I had to do something.

I had had enough of Dwayne's attitude and figured it was time to start treating him like he was treating us.

"Don't you ever change lures?" I asked.

"Sometimes. Why?" he said.

"We just trolled for two hours with two green and two orange hoochies and never had a hit. And you never tried changing to a rebel or maybe a feather?"

Knowing that he had no answer for what I just said, I figured I would let the whole matter drop. I wasn't out to bust his chops; I just wanted to make a point and the point was made.

After all the poles were in and secure in the pole holders, we took a Loran reading and set course for the Wreck. It was a nice day and the ride was just downright enjoyable. Duffy was at the wheel and his face was a lot more relaxed. I think everyone on the boat was finally starting to unwind. It was just a spectacular day to be on the ocean.

We were roughly fourteen miles out and were clipping along at about thirty miles an hour. The boat was riding beautifully and I don't think it bounced once; it just sort of skidded across the water, never leaving the tops of the waves, which were very small. Part of enjoying a boat ride like this is that you can cover a lot of area looking for feeding fish or for birds feeding on what the fish are eating.

When we were about twenty-three miles out, we were in blue water, which meant we had gotten into deeper water. The water was very clear and visibility was excellent.

Art was the first to spot something. At first, it was a couple of birds diving down and then flying up again. As Duffy slowed the boat down and turned to go in the direction of the birds, I ran to the back of the boat to see what kind of tackle he had in the box. When I opened the lid, I smiled. I could see that Duffy wasn't kidding about buying everything. I grabbed a six-inch surface Rebel. When I turned around, Dwayne was standing behind me.

Trying to patch up any hard feelings we might have, I said, "Why don't we try a Rebel on one?"

He snapped back, "I was going to."

I turned around to see how Duffy was doing and noticed a very large school of fish in front of us. Just to be on the safe side, I stopped working on setting the lines and went back to Duffy, who had that tense look back on his face.

"How should I handle this?" he said, not taking his eyes off the school of fish.

Art, who was at the front of the boat, came walking by, heading for the stern. I said to him, "I don't know what they are, but they're really feeding good. Can you help Dwayne set the lines? Put a Rebel on and leave the hoochies on the outside."

"You got it," Art said.

Duffy nervously asked again, "What should I do? Do you want to take it?"

I have been in this position many times before and it's hard to explain the excitement that's in the air.

"If all goes right, in a few minutes you'll have all the action you want."

It always seems as if there's never enough time to prepare everything and everybody seems to be in a hurry. Believe it or not, I always compare this atmosphere to that of getting concrete delivered. Everyone waits around for the truck to get there and, when it finally does, there never seems to be enough guys or time to get everything done.

I said to Duffy, "Whatever you do, don't cut through the school. Just troll around the outside about fifty feet from the ripples."

"Which way? Left or right?"

"Either," I said. "Try different speeds as you go, but whatever you do, don't cut across or the fish will scatter."

We were on the school and just waiting for the poles to snap. I ran to the front of the boat and pulled out the small casting pole I had brought. I pulled the lid to my tackle box open and looked frantically for a diamond jig – the biggest I could find. I fumbled to get the clasp closed, then looked back at the other guys, who were only inches away from the poles. I stood up and cast into the rippling water. I gave the jig a minute to sink and started trying to snag some of whatever was being eaten by the bigger fish.

The first cast drew a blank and before I cast again, I heard one of the drags on the other reels sound out. Dwayne grabbed the pole and started pulling in our first fish. Duffy started to slow down and Art, who was right behind him, yelled out, "Keep it going for a minute."

Duffy put the trolling speed back to where it was and, in less than a minute, the other pole snapped down and the drag was singing. Duffy was smiling from ear to ear and I yelled to him, "They're all ours, too. There's not another boat in sight."

As I took one more cast with the diamond jig, I yelled back to Duffy, "Slow down while we bring them in. I'll gaff or net them. You keep your eyes on the school so we don't lose them."

"How are they fighting?" I yelled back to Art and Dwayne.

"Whatever it is, they're tough!" Art hollered.

Dwayne called over, "Here comes mine. You can probably get it with a net. It's a tuna."

I wasn't halfway back to the area where Dwayne was when I saw his fish. As I walked by Duffy, who was still looking a little tense, I said, "Don't lose them. You're doing a good job."

Dwayne brought the fish up next to the boat. I looked down and said, "Bonita."

"What?" said Dwayne, as he turned his head to look at me.

I repeated, "Bonita... that's what you're catching."

Just then, Dwayne's pole went out another twenty feet or so. "Go, baby, go!" he yelled. It was the first friendly reaction I had seen come out of him.

I put the net down to look for Duffy's tackle box and yelled back to Dwayne, "Let me know when you're ready for the net." As I went through the box, I knew exactly what I was looking for and got them – feathers – two blue, two red, both had a little white in them.

"Here he comes!" cried Dwayne. I stood up and grabbed the net, looking over the side of the boat. I saw a nice sized bonita lying on its side. The fish was about eight to ten pounds and fit into the net easily. As soon as I netted the fish, I dumped it out onto the deck. The minute it hit, it started slapping the deck with its tail, which could be felt the entire length of the boat.

"Give a shout when you're ready, Art."

I said to Dwayne, "Here, put one of these feathers on."

He lost all of his friendliness and said, "Why?"

Still trying to avoid hard feelings, I said, "Because I know what I'm talking about, so will you please do it?"

"I'm ready!" yelled Art.

As I stepped around Dwayne, I could see Art's fish and, half-hanging out of the boat on my side, I netted him. Then, with the net still in the water with the fish in it, I handed it to Art. He laughed and said, "Go ahead. I'll get this."

With the two bonita in the boat, Duffy gave a little gas to the engines and steered in the direction of the school of fish that had moved away from us while we were boating the hooked fish. We were coming up on them and had changed the lures to all feathers.

I went up to Duffy and asked if he was ready for a break. He said, "No" and asked again what he should do.

"Do what you just did back there."

Duffy pulled around to try and troll across the front of the school while we waited at the poles, one by one, until all four were bent over with the sounds of set drags running from the hooked fish on the other end. Duffy stopped the boat and grabbed a line.

Within ten minutes we had all four fish in the boat. We tried to locate the school again, but couldn't find it. We had spent more time looking for the school of fish than we should have. It was time to head in.

We were moving along at a pretty good rate of speed. At this time of day, it's always hard to return because you're heading into the sun, which is reflecting off of the water, making it very hard to keep your eyes in the direction you're traveling. But land soon appeared and, within minutes, we could start to make out landmarks.

It was at this point that Duffy slowed the boat down. Then he turned his baseball cap around with Dwayne following suit.

I looked over at Art and said, "Time to wake up, buddy."

"I think you're right," he said, starting to position himself for a rough ride.

I turned around and looked at Duffy, who just smiled and said, "Hold on."

I really don't think I can describe what happened next, but I'll try. In what seemed like an explosion, the boat roared into the air. We got hit with noise from the engines and wind from the speed we were just thrown into. Suddenly, more excitement entered the fishing trip. I was thinking at any minute it would let up, but it didn't. It seemed never to let up. We just went faster and faster. I had never gone that fast on the water in my life. I tried to look at Art, but decided to get control of my own situation. The only thing I could compare it to would be going down the expressway in a convertible with four flat tires at about sixty-five miles an hour. I was so surprised by the power and speed of the boat that I couldn't wait to talk to someone about it. Right now, though, that was out of the question. It seemed like Duffy had just opened it up and we were already at the rock pile.

As the boat started to slow down, I looked over toward Art. He yelled out, "I lost my glasses!"

"I'll get them."

I saw Art's glasses on the deck, just out of reach. I let go of my grip and rolled off my seat, crawling toward them. The minute I did this, I felt the boat slow and the motors throttle back.

"You okay?" yelled Duffy, as I reached the glasses. With that, he cut the engines way back.

"Art dropped his glasses."

"I did not," he said. "They were blown off!"

"How fast were we going?"

Duffy smiled and said, "I still had about a half inch left on the throttle."

"This boat is unbelievable," I said. "You could probably make the canyon in about an hour and a half."

About a hundred miles off the southern coast of New Jersey, there is a renowned fishing spot referred to as the canyons. It's not an easy area to reach, but once you get there, the rewards are worth it. The canyons are a series of underwater abysses, formed when the Continental Shelf dropped off into the Continental Slope, creating miles of deep water that attract tuna, swordfish, marlin and other big fish. Because of their distance from shore, a trip to the canyons is a serious undertaking, requiring planning and extra efforts to make the nearly four hour journey.

"So, when we going?" was Duffy's reply.

"How about next week?" I said, with a touch of seriousness in my voice.

This was music to my ears. I was thinking about the extra hours of fishing time you could have at the canyons because of the travel time saved. The worst thing about standard canyon trips is the time it takes to get there. My sickness was starting up and I hadn't even gotten over this trip, which turned out better than I ever expected, thanks to a school of bonita.

As I pulled up in front of my house, I noticed my three daughters playing in the side yard. I stepped out of the truck and just watched them come running toward me. Every thought in my mind left and all I could see were these beautiful children that God had blessed me with running at me.

My wife and I had been attending a home bible study which had changed our lives. Both my wife and I had accepted Jesus Christ as our Lord and Savior and had made quite a few adjustments in our lives and the way we saw things. In the past, I would have had no problem popping a couple of cold ones or stopping off at a tap room for a couple of hours to talk about the day's trip. I would have missed this greeting, which I considered a blessing.

CHAPTER FOUR

I always share my fishing stories with my wife and this trip was no exception. As we finished dinner and were cleaning up, the phone rang, which started a stampede of my three daughters racing to the phone. Lisa, my oldest daughter, almost always won and came into the kitchen with a victory smile as she talked on the phone. "It's Uncle Lloyd for Daddy." She said goodbye and handed the phone to me.

Lloyd was my brother-in-law who owned his own marina in Wildwood. He informed me that next weekend he was sponsoring a shark tournament and that if I was interested he had a boat I could use. The tournament was Saturday. He then went on to say that Barb and the girls were welcome to come down and spend the day with his kids and Marie, my sister. This invitation had 'good time' written all over it.

"Sounds great. Can I check with Barb and call you back?"

"No problem. Just let me know so I can have the boat ready for you."

As I hung up the phone, I turned around to my wife, who knew something was up when she heard me say I would check with her. I explained everything to her and she was good with the idea, which meant that she and the girls would spend the day on the beach and boardwalk, then come back to the marina for the weigh-in and barbeque.

I called Lloyd back and made plans, plus got all the info on the boat he had for me. Then I called my father-in-law, Fred, to invite him, knowing before I even called him that he would say yes. It was good to talk to him. He was the only man I knew who loved fishing more than I did.

The boat we would be going on was only twenty-four feet long, which meant that if we had any more than three people the

54

boat would be over-crowded. The first person who came to mind was Duffy because I had told him about Fred and what a good shark fisherman he was. Duffy had asked me if the opportunity ever came up, he'd love to fish with Fred. I called Duffy to see if he wanted to go with us. He was glad and accepted as soon as he heard Fred was going.

I picked up all the chum and bait we needed, along with all the gear for a shark trip. We planned on leaving early, which meant Fred and I would drive down in my van and Duffy would follow us down to Wildwood in his car. Barb and the girls would come down later.

There was lots of action at the marina and Lloyd had everything ready for us. We were loaded up and on our way faster than I ever thought we could be.

The sun was up and the sea was just right as we headed out into the ocean. We had decided to run about three hours out and then set up by starting our chum slick. We had action almost from the time we got set up to when we finally hooked and brought in a nice size mako shark.

Duffy had a really good time and it seemed like he was very relaxed. It was a great day of fishing and, when we returned, we got the fish weighed-in; it was two hundred twenty-five pounds, good enough for second place in the tournament. Duffy, Fred and I had a really great time. We met up with Barb and Marie for the barbeque that followed the tournament and it turned out to be a wonderful family day.

We got home late, carried the kids into bed and made promises to do nothing but relax after church the next day. Then I went out to finish unloading the truck.

I was carrying the mako steaks out to the freezer in the garage and Barb was holding the door open for me. As I passed her she asked, "So when's the big canyon trip?"

In the past, if I made one or two canyon trips a year, I usually had enough tuna steaks to last a year. I wasn't expecting too much resistance on this trip. Plus, I had just signed two big contracts that would keep my building company busy all winter.

"I'll find out tomorrow."

Going over the day's events and then mentioning the possibility of a new trip really had my fishing sickness stirred up all over again.

Monday morning, around ten o'clock, I called Duffy's office and spoke with his secretary, who wouldn't stop talking about everything Duffy told her about the trip. I asked if he had mentioned anything about going to the canyons.

"He did," she said. "And he left a message for you that he would call you tonight with some plans."

I hung up the phone and began to fantasize about the extra time we would have fishing out there. It was nearing the end of the season and time was starting to become a factor as far as offshore fishing was concerned. Plus, there would be a lot of set-up and planning to be done.

It was late in the afternoon and I was working on Jeff's house, which was nearing completion. I was surprised when Duffy pulled up to the job site. As I walked out to meet him, the window popped open in the back of his Blazer.

"What's up," I asked him, as he got out and headed to the open window.

"Know anything about reels?"

"Yeah, they cost a lot."

"Look at these babies," he said, pulling open a small box.

"Man, they're nice!"

"I bought two of them. I figure I'll wait until winter and get two more when they go on sale."

"What about the canyon trip? Are we on?"

"What do you think I got these bad boys for?"

I could see that Duffy had the same sickness I had. The countdown for a canyon trip had begun for both of us. Duffy said I could invite Art and another guy if I wanted to, then mentioned he was inviting his son and Dwayne.

"That's perfect," I said. "I'll sit down tonight and make a list of everything we might need. What day do you want to go – and don't forget it has to be two days in case the first day is a blowout."

"Let me look at my calendar. I'll call you at home tonight."

Duffy was really excited about the trip and, as he pulled away, I couldn't stop thinking about it. On top of the extra fishing time, I also got to invite Art and another friend. Duffy wasn't even out of sight and I had started putting the tools away. I stopped by Art's on the way home and gave him a heads-up on everything but the date, which I didn't know yet.

"Just let me know as soon as you can."

When I got home, I called my brother-in-law, Bill, and asked if he would like to go. I was sure he would be up for a trip. I asked if he had been out fishing lately.

"No, why? You got anything going on?"

"How about a canyon trip next week?"

"Next week? I can't. I go to school in Trenton for two weeks, starting Monday. Who are you going with?"

Not only did Bill know Duffy, but he had a story about Duffy and his last boat.

"Well, last year, after a party, Duffy took some friends out for a ride in his speed boat. When he returned, he misjudged the dock and crashed into it and his neighbor's boat. From what I heard, he smashed it up pretty good."

"Look, I'm just telling you what I heard. Besides, that sounds like a nice rig he has now. Man, I wish I could go, but they only offer this course twice a year. If I don't go now, I'll have to take the course in December and then I won't be able to go deer hunting."

As I hung up the phone, I thought to myself that I should give it a little time and think about who else to invite. I decided I would wait before I called anyone.

Not five minutes after I had hung up with Bill did the next person come to mind - Joe Walls. Not only is Joe Walls a good fisherman, but he's also a lot of fun to be around. One of the other reasons for my choice was that he kept his boat at Hackney's.

One of the funniest fishing trips I ever went on was in Joe's boat just one year ago. It was the Lions Club Annual Bluefish Tournament and he invited me to go on his boat. You didn't have to be an official Lions member. I remembered that Joe and I were the only two on the boat who didn't get seasick. The other three guys didn't even like fishing, but were going out of loyalty for the Lions Club.

It was foggy on the day of the tournament and, as we left the check-in dock with the "okay" to fish, we started for the inlet with very poor visibility. Our plan was to just troll the stone beds, which are about four miles off the Ocean City beach. As we passed the rock pile and took a compass reading for the stone beds, we noticed that our crew was already turning green. I don't think I'd ever seen the ocean that calm. There was no wind and the fog was getting thicker. The farther we went, the worse it got and when visibility got to about one hundred feet, Joe stopped the boat and said, "I think we ought to wait this out."

"Not a bad idea – we're only a few miles off and maybe the wind will pick up and clean this stuff up."

Not two minutes after we stopped, one of the guys in the back got sick. Both Joe and I knew it was just a matter of time before the other two caught up to him; he was hanging over the side of the boat.

While we thought about what to do next, the fog got worse. We couldn't see fifty feet in front of us. Joe's boat had no electronic gear, so we could only figure approximately where we were. We finally came to the decision that we would drop the lines and troll toward the stone beds. After trolling awhile, we made a large turn and started heading back in the direction we had just come from. The fog was still thick and, the way it looked, the three guys in the back were planning a mutiny.

Just when we thought it couldn't get worse, Joe slowed the boat down and said, "What the heck is that?"

Both of us strained our eyes at the object in the fog in front of us. "Oh, my God! It's a fishing pier!" Joe said.

With that, one of the guys in the back came up to Joe and said, "I think we ought to head in now, Joe."

Joe, who is a very funny man, answered, "That might not be as easy as it sounds."

"What do you mean by that?" said the guy, ready to argue with Joe.

"Well, we're just a little lost."

"Why don't you call the Coast Guard?"

Then one of the other fellows came up to the cabin, which was now starting to fill up with people. He said, "Why not just ask that guy over there?"

"What guy? Over where?" said Joe, putting the boat in neutral.

"On the surfboard."

Sure enough, about thirty feet away was a young blonde-haired kid sitting on a surfboard, watching us in our dilemma.

"Sounds like a winner to me," said Joe.

I pulled the lines in while Joe turned the boat around and slowly pulled the boat over toward the surfer, who looked expressionlessly at us. Joe turned the engines off and the sound of breaking waves could be heard. He was a little concerned, but not enough that he couldn't add a little fun to this situation. As we floated near the surfer, Joe left the cabin and walked out on the deck, looking at the young man, who was still just watching us.

"Hey, how's the surf?" Joe asked.

The surfer just said, "Not bad."

"Would you like a cold soda?"

"No," replied the surfer.

"You wouldn't happen to know what pier that is, would you?"

I was in the cabin, laughing my head off because Joe was being very dry about how he asked the questions.

The surfer was getting annoyed at Joe and snapped back, "It's the fishing pier, why?"

"Is that Ocean City?" asked Joe.

"Look, man, where are you guys from?"

Joe was in the middle of explaining that we were in the Lions Annual Bluefish Tournament and had gotten lost in the fog, when one of the men in the cabin came running out and bent over the side, right in front of Joe and the surfer.

The surfer just yelled, "Oh, man, that's gross!" and started paddling toward shore.

Joe yelled out, "You haven't seen any bluefish about, have you?"

I can write this story, but it really was one of those things that if you were there, you would know just how very funny it was. Anyway, we followed the coastline back and that was the end of that trip, with the exception that Joe asked me if I ever had room for him on a canyon trip to please call him. He knows Art and we all get along. 'Boy,' I thought, 'This trip was going to be great!'

🐋🐋🐋🐋🐋🐋

As I entered the living room, I smelled something good and went right to the kitchen to find my wife in the midst of cooking dinner. Barb was talking on the phone and I startled her.

"Oh, Gail, I'll call you later," she said. She hung up the phone, smiled, kissed me and said, "You're home early. Anything wrong?"

"No, just finished up and didn't want to start anything new."

"There's a letter for you."

When I picked it up and started to open it, Barb said, "It's an invitation to a party. Don't you want to know how I know?"

I answered, "Yeah, how did you know?"

"Duffy's secretary called and apologized for it being such short notice, but wants us to try and make it."

"What do you want to do?" I asked.

"Well, I've been talking to Gail. Did you know they know Duffy?"

"Yeah, Bill mentioned it to me. Seems he's quite a party guy. I don't know that much about him. All we've ever done was go fishing together."

"Well, just make sure that's all you do. He's been married and has a reputation of being a playboy."

"It's like I said – I just fished with him and to tell you the truth, I don't really want to go to the party. How about you?"

"Not particularly, but I'll do whatever you want me to do."

I asked Barb if she was finished with the phone and was questioned adamantly as to who I was going to call. As a joke, I said, "To confirm the party invitation, why?" It didn't get a laugh.

"I'm going to call Joe Walls up and invite him on the trip."

"That's a great idea," Barb said as she forgot about my not-so-funny joke. "Joe is like Art and I don't know anyone who doesn't like him.

I called Joe and he was at home.

"I've got a good trip lined up if you're interested."

"What is it?" he asked.

"A chunking tuna trip to the canyon."

"How much?" was his next question.

"Just share the expenses – it's not a charter."

"I'm in. When is it?"

"Next week. I'll call you with details as soon as I get them. Are you sure you're in?"

"You better believe it. Thanks!" he said.

I hung up the phone and, not ten seconds later, the phone rang.

It was Joe, who said, "Look, I was so excited about the trip, I forgot to ask how Barb and the kids are."

"They're all fine. How's Janet and your kids?"

"Good, good. Do me a favor? Call as soon as you know so I can get the day off."

Joe is a bank executive. Actually, I have done a lot of business with Joe and, wisely enough, we never mention business when we go fishing.

Duffy called and explained that he'd be in touch after the weekend because he had to prepare for the party and was sorry we weren't coming.

After I hung up with Duffy, my wife came into my office and said, "Look, you're getting a lot of fishing time in and it doesn't look like its slowing down for you. How about a little family time?"

That was fine with me. I don't think she expected me to just drop everything, but I stood up and said, "You're right." I called Art and Joe, then turned off the light in my office and just spent the next two days with my family. With no date set for the trip, it was easier to overcome my sickness and, to tell you the truth, I almost forgot about going until the fishing report came out Sunday morning.

The offshore fishing was at its peak, according to *The Press*. Swordfish, yellow fin, with good catches of long fin albacore. All of a sudden, I couldn't wait. Duffy must have read it, too, because when we came home from church there was a message from him.

I called Duffy, who confessed that he had read the paper, then hit me with some really bad news. It turned out the only day he could make it was next Sunday. I was the only one that had a problem with it. Art was happy he didn't have to reschedule patients, Joe didn't have to take the day off. Me, I lose my family day and skip church, not to mention that Monday was my wife's birthday.

I hung up the phone and shared the bad news with my wife. At first, she was very upset. I couldn't blame her. Sunday was our family day and we all looked forward to it each week. I didn't know what to do when my wife said to go ahead and go. I sincerely did regret it and was feeling bad about it. I told her this would be the last trip of the year.

She said, "Yeah, unless they're really biting again." Then she said, "Just bring back some tuna for my birthday."

During the week, a few small problems came up. There was a shortage of bait and it was hard to locate the three slabs of butterfish we would need, but we did it. The week went by and, before I knew it, it was Saturday, which was basically a set-up day. Almost the whole day would be spent in preparations. Everyone would meet to go over the list of things that needed to be done and to deliver all of the supplies. These would then be packed and stowed away until the trip.

I remember going over my list and checking everything I had to do, then asking Duffy to do the same with his list. Art called and confirmed that he had picked up the bait and had it in his freezer. Everything was packed with the exception of the poles, bait and lunch. Duffy and Dwayne had plotted out our course of action based on the fishing report and everything seemed ready to go.

The weather for Sunday was a promising forecast. It was going to blow out of the northwest at fifteen to twenty miles an hour, with winds tapering off as the day went on until about noon, when the winds would change to southwest. Seas were to be three to four feet, dropping to two feet or less by mid afternoon.

It was now late afternoon and Duffy asked me if I would like to go out for dinner.

"No, I'm sure my wife is making dinner. By the way, she's a little upset over the fact that we're going on a Sunday."

Duffy had little sympathy for me as he laughed and said, "That's one of those things I don't miss about being married."

There was nothing left to do but go home and try to get some rest before the trip.

CHAPTER FIVE

When I got home, I walked in to find a fully set table, missing the food and people needed to complete the scene.

"I thought we'd have our Sunday dinner tonight because you're not going to be here to have it with us tomorrow night," my wife said. This was my first clue that booking a trip on a Sunday was not an unforgivable sin.

I sat down to dinner and was treated like the guest of honor. I couldn't say anything else except, "I'm going to miss you guys tomorrow and I promise I won't go on Sundays anymore."

My apology seemed to be accepted by my girls, who were talking over each other, asking me question after question about the trip. "What time are you leaving?" "Will you wake us up to say goodbye?" "What will you catch?" "Will you see any whales?"

If I didn't know better, I'd think that they were going; they were so excited about it. After dinner, I had a few phone calls to make, one of them to the weather station for an update on the weather and then try to get some rest.

With the alarm set, van packed, everything I could think of taken care of, I went to bed in hopes of falling asleep, if only for an hour. I'd be satisfied with just lying down in bed for a few hours.

As I laid in bed drifting off to sleep, I began to dream about a successful offshore trip I had been on several years ago...

The sun was blinding as it reflected off the surface of the rolling waves, and the constant rumble of the diesel engines never fluctuated as we trolled through the crystalline blue waters. Except for a small white marlin that had slapped at our baits earlier, there had been no action since the sun came up. It was midday and we were all trying to stay positive and not think about getting skunked. After all the planning and effort put into this offshore trip, nobody wanted to go home without at least one knockdown and hookup.

Our lines were laid out in a perfect trolling pattern with two sets of teasers hopping madly in and out of the white foamy backwash of the boat. Almost a mile away, unbeknownst to us, feeding frantically, a large blue marlin slashes his long bill with lightning-like strikes at balls of bait fish just under the surface of the smooth rolling ocean. The approaching drone of the diesels seems to intensify his feeding frenzy.

There were no sightings of birds feeding or other surface activity, so we had no reason to expect a strike on our lines. We all stared at the baits being dragged behind the boat, trying to will a fish to come up and attack one of them. Except for an occasional roll of the boat that caused a rattling sound from the holding clips on the outriggers, nothing was happening. We were mesmerized by the constant drone of the engines, the hot sun and the steady rolling of the boat as we trolled on. The ocean was calm, the weather was beautiful... a perfect day for fishing.

Diving to a lower depth at the sight and sound of the approaching hull, without sensing any immediate danger, the large marlin is suddenly attracted by the sight of the multi-colored lures bouncing in the wake of the boat. Natural hunting instincts start to take over as the fish turns and races to follow the baits, darting left then right and becoming more and more excited by the appearance of different lures and the white water churned up by the two eighteen-inch propellers.

The magnificent fish is swimming faster now and moving closer to the surface, trailing the outside lure and, with little effort, is well within striking distance. The sound of the engines and the movement of the baits is stirring him into a frenzy and, with a burst of speed, the fish attacks the outside bait, knocking it out of the water. He turns sharply behind the boat and, as the second set of lures passes by, he spots his prey and closes his jaws tightly over the lure. His attempt to scatter the baits is instantly forgotten as the large sharpened steel hook pushes its way through the lower corner of his jaw.

As he feels the resistance caused by the line and pole, his hunting instincts are turned off and he is now in full survival mode. He turns away from the boat and dives deep, peeling line off the reel almost effortlessly. He knows he's in for the fight of his life.

On the deck of the boat, the once serene and monotonous scene is transformed into one of chaos in seconds. The outrigger whips back uncontrollably as the clip snaps free and the line is released. For a second, the drag on the outside reel starts to sound.

Everyone comes to life as the shout of "Fish on!" is followed by an explosion of activity on deck. Just as someone picks up the outside line and realizes it was only a knockdown, the second reel bends and starts screaming as line is peeled off at an alarming rate.

I lift the pole from the holder and point the tip in the direction of the fleeing fish, adjust the tension on the drag and set the hook with one firm pull upward. The straps of the fighting vest are drawn tight around my back by one of the mates and, as I slide into the fighting chair, the rod is pulled to me and placed between my legs, into the metal gimbal. As I feel the tension on the line, I release the drag slightly. Helping hands clip the vest straps to the reel and I feel the rod become part of my forearm while I strain to keep the tip of the rod up.

There is chaos all around me as the other lines are unclipped and reeled in as fast as possible to prevent any tangles. The motors are backed off and the noise of all the other reels being cranked in and put out of the way can be heard. My thumb has not left the slide drag since it was put in my hand. At this point, nothing can be done to control the amount of line being taken by the fish. I can only try to prevent a backlash.

At a depth of one hundred and fifty feet, with the sun's rays still filtering through the blue water, the fish continues on his power run, peeling yet more line from the spool. The deeper he goes, the more he starts to feel the increase of the drag caused by all that line and he begins to turn slightly from his original escape route. As he does so, he is burning energy that has been stored for his survival. His head starts to tilt from the constant drag and he begins to turn even more, sensing a decrease in the tension on the line.

As the fish starts to circle, the captain powers down the boat and keeps the fighting chair facing the direction of the fish, all the while shouting out directions and encouragement to keep the slack out of the line. There has been no gain in line to this point and we all realize this is a very large fish. The line has finally stopped peeling out and, for the first time since the fish has been hooked, I am able to reel in small amounts of line with little resistance. That doesn't last long.

The fish begins to feel the pressure increase and makes another run, this time heading straight for the bottom, peeling off more line like it was nothing. He's getting to the depth of water where the sun's rays are rapidly diminishing and is exerting extremely large amounts of energy.

I reset the drag to put more pressure on the fish and prevent him from spooling off all the line. My arms are aching now and, with the reel clipped to the fighting vest, I try to shift some of the pressure to my back and shoulders. Finally, the spool starts to slow and the continuous loss of line turns into short bursts of line being removed... with an occasional stop. Ever so slightly, I increase the drag as the run comes to an end and the fish starts to turn again. Five cranks of the reel and the fish takes a short burst of line out, then just lays on it. He's beginning to wear down ever so much.

Feeling that the run is over, I adjust the drag slightly again and begin cranking the reel, finally replacing some of the line that he has taken off. Again, that doesn't last long as he peels off another fifty yards in seconds. Back and forth we go, gaining and losing line like we were on a see-saw. I'm really beginning to feel the fatigue in my arms, shoulders, back and now legs. This thing is a tank.

The boat is now in neutral and is rolling slightly with the swell. The sun is bright and hot and there is little to no breeze. Sweat is streaming from every pore in my body and my clothes are soaked with perspiration. Just keeping the rod tip up and cranking the reel every so often is a major effort. The chair doesn't feel as comfortable as it did and the fighting vest is pulling on my shoulders where it meets my back. There is a constant burning sensation in both arms as I reel in line every chance I get.

Still, there is no sight of the fish but line is being gained as he continues to swim in a circular pattern. It feels as if the action has slowed as I bring him closer to the surface. I realize, very quickly, this is only an illusion.

The fish is now swimming into the sun's rays and, to avoid the blinding light, turns sharply, feeling the decrease in pressure of the line immediately. Sensing freedom is at hand, he turns again and heads for the surface at Mach I speed and explodes through the silver surface of the sea, becoming totally airborne, all the while shaking its massive head and whipping its body and tail rapidly, while rotating in slow motion, trying to shake the hook and gain his release. What a magnificent sight he is.

As he becomes airborne, there is slack in the line and the pole snaps back to straight, no longer bent from the pressure of the fish. There is a split second where I think I may have lost him but I begin cranking in the line anyway, redirecting it back on the spool. Everyone is staring in the direction of the fish, hoping he hasn't thrown the hook, while I furiously crank the reel trying to remove all the slack.

As the fish hits the surface, he creates a tremendously large splash, disappears for a second and then launches into the air again. Trying not to be distracted by his acrobatics, I continue to crank the reel rapidly, finally beginning to feel some tension on the line again. The fish must feel it, too, because he turns and peels off fifty yards with ease.

I sense a turning point has been reached. Although he has taken fifty yards of line rapidly, he turns sideways again and allows me to recover most of it just as quickly. His runs become shorter and shorter and his jumps not so high and acrobatic. I'm finally wearing him down.

The crew is watching closely and is excited by the size of him and the show the fish has put on. After what seems like hours later, but is really only minutes, someone spots the leader coming out of the water. This means the fish is close.

Leather gloves are put on and a tag is prepared to stick in the fish. It was agreed before leaving the dock that all billfish caught would be tagged and released to fight another day. This one has certainly earned his freedom. As the snap swivel clicks at the tip of the pole, the mate starts to pull the wire leader, leading the fish close alongside the boat, being careful not to kink the wire and aware that the fish could still make another run. Once next to the boat, the captain appears with the tagging stick, inserting the tag while the fish is photographed, measured and the hook removed.

I rush over and run my hand over the back of this magnificent monster of the deep, thanking him for the experience of a lifetime, while the mate lets the bill go and, with half a flip of its tail, it pulls away from the boat, takes one look at us and disappears into the deep blue waters once again.

As I dried off the hand that had just touched the fish, I realized what an accomplishment it was to hook, land and tag a fish of this size. It doesn't always work out that way and that's what keeps us coming back. You just never know what's going to happen. That's why we do what we do...

The next thing I knew, the alarm rang and in one shifting motion of my arm I reached over and turned the switch to play music instead of the loud buzz.

I was up and standing next to the bed when Barb, in a sleepy voice, said, "Is it that time already?"

"Yes," I answered. "Why don't you stay in bed while I get ready?" But she was already up and headed for the kitchen.

I had showered and finished dressing before going to the kitchen, the only lighted room in the house. I could smell the coffee way before I got there and, as I entered the room, I stopped to stare at my wife who was wrapping sandwiches. As I put my arms around her, trying to be loving, she elbowed me and said, "I'm really upset with you about fishing on a Sunday."

"You know I had no control over that."

"I know, but it still upsets me."

She elbowed me again and said, "Let go, I have to finish your lunch."

"Not until you say you love me."

"You know I love you, now let go. So where are you going and when will you be home?"

"You know, I don't know. Duffy and Dwayne planned everything. But we should be home before dark. I'll call you in plenty of time to come over. Why don't you pick up Art's wife when you come?"

I gave her instructions on how to get to Duffy's house. I love to meet my wife and kids at the dock so they can see what we caught.

I was running right on schedule and was nearing my departure time from home. I sipped on a cup of coffee and finished loading the van. I came back to the kitchen only to find Barb had moved into the next room and had fallen asleep on the couch.

I bent down to kiss her and she awoke with a start. "Don't forget to kiss the kids goodbye and try not to wake them."

The hallway was well-lit with nightlights, as were the bedrooms. It was dark, but my eyes were well adjusted and I could see each one of them. This was something I never rushed and always enjoyed. I never woke them, but I must confess that sometimes I just sat and stared at them.

I turned around to head toward the front door and saw Barb standing in the hallway, watching me. As I came out, she said to me in a whisper, "They ought to kick you, but instead they worship you."

With that, I assured her, no more Sunday trips. I walked her back to our bedroom and kissed her goodbye.

"Please be careful. And call us as soon as you get in, not after you wash down."

It was three-thirty in the morning and the night air was refreshing, the stars lit up the sky and I could feel energy coming into my body.

Getting into the van, I could see Barb had gotten out of bed and was now on the porch to wave good-bye. I turned the interior light on and blew her a kiss as I pulled away.

I knew, as I headed for Art's, that he would be up. He was not only up, but out in the driveway standing next to his fishing gear. I backed into his driveway and heard him say, "You're right on time."

I turned the motor off and slid down off the seat. Smiling, I said, "Are you surprised?"

I started loading the van while Art returned to his house to give his wife Anna her kiss good-bye. Anna peeked her head out of the door just long enough to say, "Hi, Dave."

I replied with a "Hi, Anna," and mentioned to her that Barb was going to bring our kids over to Duffy's after we got in and, if she was interested, to call Barb; she had all the directions and they could probably go together if she wanted.

Anna laughed, "What if you don't catch anything?"

I just laughed and asked, "When are you going back to sleep?"

Art gave her his kiss good-bye and was getting into the passenger seat of the van. When I got in, Art said, "This is going to be great. I haven't been able to think of anything all week except this trip."

As far as we were concerned, the trip was officially started. The next stop was Joe's house and then on to Duffy's. When we pulled up in front of Joe's, only the living room light was on. Both Art and I walked up to the door, wondering if Joe was even awake because it seemed like there should have been a little more activity than what was going on. We opened the storm door and were just about to knock when the porch light went on and the door opened.

"You had us scared there for a minute, Joe. We thought you were sleeping."

"What? Are you kidding?" he said. "Listen, do me a favor. Janet's asleep. I don't want to wake her."

We went into our silent mode.

It was really good to see Joe and Art were as excited about the trip as I was. It sort of guaranteed a good mood. We all discussed the weather forecast while heading over to Duffy's.

Pulling up to Duffy's house, I was a little surprised to see the light on and the door wide open. We each grabbed something and headed for the door that passed under Duffy's house and out to the dock where the boat was. Upon entering the back yard, we were blinded momentarily by the light that Duffy had on the dock and on the house. No one was on the boat, so I instructed Art and Joe to continue unloading the van and just leave everything on the dock until we were ready to organize it on the boat.

We stood there looking at the boat shining in the light. Joe said, "That is one beautiful rig."

Art turned to Joe, "Wait until you feel what it's like when he opens it up."

We headed back toward the house and, at the end of the dock, I turned and headed for the stairs that led up to the house where I expected to find Duffy, his son, and Dwayne. As soon as I came to the top step I could hear music and now could see Duffy in the kitchen making sandwiches.

"What's up?" I yelled.

He looked up and smiled. "Looks like we're going to have a good day," he said.

"Are you just about ready?"

He sort of frowned a little and said, "I can't get a hold of my son. He's either on the way or forgot about the trip."

"Well, maybe by the time we get the boat loaded, he'll be here."

"I don't know," moaned Duffy. "I've been calling for an hour. He probably forgot. I haven't talked to him since Wednesday. I should have called him yesterday."

Art and Joe were unloading the van. Duffy mentioned that he and Dwayne had most of their packing done already, plus what we had packed earlier. I figured I would grab a cup of coffee and hopefully use the bathroom before the trip.

Duffy laughed and said, "You better tell Dwayne to use the exhaust fan. He's been in there a long time."

As I poured myself a cup of coffee, Dwayne came out of the bathroom and sped out to the dock almost unnoticed. I took a sip of coffee and turned toward the bathroom. Before I could get within reach of the doorknob, I realized that Dwayne hadn't used the exhaust fan and I pulled an about-face. A laugh came from Duffy, who was watching me.

"What's the matter?"

I looked at Duffy and he said, "That's why they call them shithouses."

I went back to the dock where Art, Joe and Dwayne were waiting. As I approached, I saw Dwayne climb into the boat and begin to set up for starting the engines. He lowered the engines into the water and the power lifts made an unmistakable sound. Just as the sound stopped, Dwayne moaned in a disagreeable voice, "There's no gas in the tanks."

It's not as if something like this couldn't happen, so I pulled an about-face and raced back to the house where Duffy was putting

ice in the cooler. He just turned with a smile on his face, after hearing me question him on when he had last gassed up.

"There's a separate switch for the fuel tank gauges. I capped them off yesterday afternoon after you left."

On my return to the boat, Dwayne had both engines running and still had a look of concern on his face. When I told him about the separate switches, he sighed and started flipping switches like a madman. After hitting just about all of them, he said, "There. That's more like it," as the fuel gauges moved from empty to full.

I turned around and saw Duffy coming down the dock, cooler in hand. When he reached the boat, I grabbed the cooler from him and started introducing Joe to Duffy. After they shook hands, I turned to Dwayne and asked if he had met Joe.

Art was standing next to me and said, "Yeah, I introduced them when you were checking on the fuel."

"Everything ready?" I asked.

"We're as ready as we'll ever be," Duffy said. "Let me try calling my son one more time."

After hearing Duffy leave a message, he just said, "Oh well, we can't wait any longer. It's already quarter to five."

With that said, both Art and I went to the bow and started undoing the mooring lines. Both of us turned around and looked to see if the stern was untied.

Duffy, who was at the wheel, looked up and in a funny voice said, "Is we or is we not ready?"

"We is!" was the reply from the bow. The two motors popped into gear and suddenly foam was coming from under the bow. Art and I guided the boat out, trying to keep the sides from rubbing up against the pilings, and we felt the boat being taken over by the motors.

We pulled out into the main channel and the shoreline took on an entirely different look. So did the meadow, which seemed much more distant. Traveling at night in a boat is different than in the day. I don't know if it's the sky's reflection on the water or what, but things seem to look a little farther away than they really are and, if you're not careful, you could easily run aground.

We headed toward the Ninth Street Bridge, the first of two bridges we would pass under before getting into the inlet and then the ocean.

I took a walk around the deck, just to familiarize myself with the boat again. There's something cool about walking in the opposite direction you are traveling. Plus, the view of the bridges and houses that line the channel was always enjoyable to look at. We were in a 'no-wake' zone and would be until we got to the second bridge, so it was a slow approach to our much anticipated trip.

As I walked by the center console, Duffy handed me a spotlight and asked if I would spot the up-coming channel markers and buoys. The minute I was given the spotlight, I took my job to heart. It was a really nice light and I couldn't resist flashing it on Art and Joe as they organized the front of the boat. Art had his hands over his eyes and asked if the sun had come up.

I had no problem with my job. As a matter of fact, I preferred it over any other job. I would spot the next buoy or channel marker about a quarter of a mile away and then would lower the light to a point in the front of the boat. The light would serve as a headlight, just for safety, in case of any floating debris. Occasionally, I lifted the light beam up to the on-coming markers and then back to the front of the boat.

Art and Joe were in front of the center console. Duffy was at the wheel, enjoying piloting the boat, with Dwayne next to him. The second bridge was in sight and we were closing in on it. I put the spotlight on the center span and Duffy just guided us through like it was nothing.

Entering the inlet, my job was at its peak and I had no problem handling it. It was very dark and, if you've never done it before, you could very easily panic. We could see the waves breaking on the white sandy beaches and the sky was starting to get a little pinkish color to it in the East. There was a definite change in the boat ride as the waves and currents started to rock the boat. We were all used to the engines and their constant rumble. As we passed the halfway point, Duffy gave the throttle a little push and the boat picked up speed.

We headed for the three-mile buoy, where we would check the Loran navigating system and call for a radio check. If everything checks out, it's time to run.

The sky in the East was starting to get a lot more pinkish color to it. After we got our radio check loud and clear from another boat, Duffy put the numbers into the Loran (LOng RAnge Navigation - a terrestrial radio navigation system which enables ships and aircraft to determine their position and speed from low frequency radio signals transmitted by fixed land based radio receivers using a receiver unit) and we were officially on our way. Duffy gave the throttle another push and the boat jumped up and planed off.

The wind was coming out of the Northwest, which made the water unbelievably calm. However, this would change; the farther away from land, the rougher the seas would get. The winds were expected to change and come out of the Southwest as the day went on and the seas would again flatten out. The pink area, once on the horizon, was now starting to move across the sky.

I looked to the East and saw a reddish-orange light start to appear on the horizon. It seemed almost impossible to take your eyes off of it. As the sun started to round itself from the horizon, I got sort of a sneak preview of what was ahead of us. The tips of the waves were cutting across the sun as it started rising. There was definitely rough water ahead, but there was no way of telling just how bad it would be until we got about eleven miles out. It was hard to concentrate on the seas because I kept getting caught up in the beauty of the sunrise. The night coolness had left after the sun rose in the sky.

The sun had risen high enough that it was no longer hard to make out the seas. They were rough and all I could think about was the weather report that said it would get better as the day went on. After looking at the horizon long enough to know that the ride was going to be getting rougher, I turned around to look in the direction of land. It was now completely out of sight. I was surprised because we hadn't been travelling that long, forgetting about the speed of Duffy's boat.

The sun was up now and it was time to put the spotlight away. It seemed like the wind was picking up because the spray was starting to come up over the bow after almost every wave we hit. What would happen was, the boat would hit a wave and splash water up and out, which would normally just splash away from the boat. But, the wind would pick up and hold the spray almost still and the boat would drive through the wall of water. The size of the wave determined the amount of spray we would get covered with.

It was certainly light enough to put the spotlight away and, after I passed the front of the console, I got down on all fours like a dog and began crawling the rest of the way to the forward hatch.

Passing Art and Joe, Joe laughed and said, "What's the matter, Dave? No guts to get up and walk?"

I was just about to ask Joe if he'd like to put the spotlight away when a wall of spray covered everyone but me because I was below the side of the boat. As the spray hit Art and Joe, they both gave out a yell. I changed my comeback line to, "No...I knew that was coming. Why, Joe?"

The boat was really starting to pound now and I was having a tough time getting to the forward compartment. However, with persistence and an occasional drop to the deck, I made it. As I put away the light, I looked at my duffel bag and figured this would be a good time to put the storm gear on. The minute I pulled the bright yellow suit out of the bag, I began to hear shouts from Joe, Art and Duffy, all asking me to grab their storm gear while I was there. With everyone's storm gear in hand, I turned, only to see everyone on the boat laughing at me. I started back with everyone's storm gear in one arm and it seemed to be going pretty well until I got to Art and Joe. The wave we hit really slammed us and my one arm gave out as I fell to the deck. All the laughter stopped and everyone had serious looks on their faces. When I looked up, Art was down on one knee and was helping me up. When he asked if I was alright, I laughed and said, "Yeah, I landed on the storm gear. I wasn't hurt at all."

Joe and Art started putting their suits on right away. I had put mine on before I came back. As I stood up, I grabbed at whatever was stationary and positioned myself next to Duffy at the wheel.

I leaned over and yelled, "Duffy, I think we ought to cut it back a little. We're getting pounded pretty good."

I handed Duffy the storm gear and Dwayne stepped in front of him to give him a chance to put on his suit. Before he stepped away from the wheel, Duffy ordered Dwayne to cut the engines back to where we wouldn't bounce so much.

We had made good time, even though the sea was getting unexpectedly worse. The wind, however, was just downright annoying. It made us miserable and showed no sign of letting up.

Standing next to the controls, I started to think about what was going on around us – I even had thoughts of turning around. I remembered the weather forecast - that as the day went on it would get better. We had so much into this trip that the only thing I could think of was maybe this was as bad as it would get. Duffy had returned to the wheel now and had a look of concern.

"What do you think?"

Knowing what he meant, I just said, "I thought about it and, if it doesn't get any worse, we'll be okay."

With that, Duffy slowed the boat down even more to where we were no longer getting wet. "We'll just take it easy and see what happens. If it gets any worse, we'll turn tail and head in."

"Sounds like a plan," I said.

With the boat slowed down, Art got up and came to the center console to ask, "What's going on?"

I said, "We're just going to go at a comfortable speed and, if it gets too bad, we're going to turn."

It was about a quarter to seven and we were twenty-two miles out. I began to lose hope of trolling for marlin and started to concentrate on the tuna, which was the main objective of the trip. Every now and then, a wave would send up a wall of backwash and the spray would cover the entire boat. It was a lot easier to take with storm gear on. We spotted a couple of boats on the horizon and it lifted our spirits.

We kept changing our speed in the hope of finding one that would make the trip a little easier. Within a few minutes we realized that the two boats we had spotted were headed toward us. After a few more minutes, they passed us on their way in.

Art got up from his seat again and said, "That's not a good sign, is it? Where do you think they're coming from?"

"I can only guess they spent the night at the canyon. We would have seen them earlier, when it was dark, if they had come out of Atlantic City or Ocean City. What I can't figure out is why they're coming in now."

The high opinion I had of Duffy's boat had come down a little. On top of being a wet boat, it really didn't take much of a sea to be uncomfortable in it. I have been in a lot worse than the waves we were in now, in a lot smaller boat, and had no trouble. However, no matter what we did, we couldn't seem to come to a comfortable traveling speed. The major problem was the wind; it was coming from offshore making the waves turbulent. It seemed it wasn't getting any better or worse, but one thing was for sure – it was uncomfortable.

Duffy started changing the trim tabs, making a big difference in the way the boat was riding. It raised the bow and put a little more strain on the engines, which meant we would burn a little more fuel than normal, but it really made a big difference. In just a few minutes, at the new pace, the ride was getting a little more bearable. Even the spray seemed to be a little less relentless. The wind was starting to change. I looked back in the direction of the boats we had seen heading in and I couldn't see them.

"Duffy, let's listen to the weather on the radio." With that, we switched to the right station and listened to the same promising forecast we had heard the night before.

CHAPTER SIX

We had cut our speed to a point that the spray wasn't soaking us like it was earlier. It was the first time in quite a while that we could dry our faces. It felt good to get the salt out of the corners of our eyes and feel the fresh sea air. As I took in the sights of the rolling waves all around us, I noticed Duffy waving me over to him. I made my way to the center console, keeping at least one hand on something stationary.

"What's up?" I half yelled, arriving at the center console. The sound of the motors had everyone half shouting in order to communicate with each other.

He told me, "I'm getting shocks from the trim tab switches."

I reached for the switch and laid the back of my hand on them. Sure enough, I could feel the tingling effect of a shock. It was annoying having to yell, but cutting the engines in this wind and sea would be crazy.

I asked Duffy if this had ever happened before, as I pulled a towel out from under the center console and began to dry the control panel off.

"Never," said Duffy.

"How about the rest of the panel?"

"Everything checks out okay. It's just the trim tab switches."

I wiped the panel again, then asked Duffy if they were still operating. He said that they seemed to be working fine, it was just the shocks that had him worried.

After wiping the panel again, I said to Duffy, "Look, you're the captain. You get to make the call. What time is it and how far out are we?" I asked.

Duffy replied, "It's a little past seven and we're twenty-five miles out." I knew Duffy wasn't in the mood to make a decision, but it really was his call.

"Well, we're not getting much spray at this speed and the seas aren't getting any worse. We'll keep going and see if it gets any better."

Knowing that we were going to continue, I turned and started back to the comfortable spot I had just left. Halfway there, I looked up at the bow of the boat, which was about to hit one of the biggest waves I had seen in awhile. Instinctively, I turned my back to it to avoid the soaking wall of mist that was sure to follow.

We were travelling at about eight to twelve miles an hour. I was half bent over, looking at the floor of the boat, with one hand on the rail of the center console and one hand on the padded sideboard. What followed was a lifting sensation, combined with a sudden stop, which sent all of my normal reactions into short circuit. Without warning, a wall of water hit me with such force that it took my legs out from under me. My fall was somewhat cushioned by the water as it washed me uncontrollably to the back of the boat with tremendous power. As the force of the water equalized around me and I felt like I was back in control of my body, I struggled to get to my feet. My first reaction was to see if everyone was all right. I almost panicked at the sight of the boat. I couldn't see any of the other guys and I was standing knee-deep in water.

"Where is everyone?" I shouted.

I was the first one standing and I think my voice pulled everyone out of shock because suddenly there was movement and voices all about the deck, which still had a foot and a half of water on it. The water on the deck was a shock but, I can honestly say, the silence of the motors was an even bigger shock. I looked around again and tried to distinguish and count the men on the deck.

I yelled, "Is everyone all right?"

I heard three of them yell, "Yes," and a slow, "Yeah, I'm all right," from Art.

Everyone was stunned and adjusting to the situation in their own way. Dwayne stood up next to me and tried to start the engines.

The windshield was gone and the center console was completely exposed. I picked up a five-gallon bucket and started bailing water. I really thought I was doing a good job until the next wave broke over the transom of the boat. This wave went the entire length of the boat, tossing me as it pushed by. It was at this moment I knew that what I was doing was hopeless. The water was now up to my waist as I headed to the back of the boat to find the surprise of a lifetime. The transom to which the motors were mounted was about two feet under water, which meant the boat was sinking.

I turned and saw Dwayne had picked up the radio mike and had started to issue a 'May Day' call for help. I moved back to the center console to give Dwayne our Loran location. Just as I got back to look at the screen, a foot of water covered it and I saw that it was darkened.

* *

COAST GUARD REPORT

AT 7:17 A.M., COAST GUARD THIRD DISTRICT TELECOMMUNICATIONS CENTER RECEIVES A MAYDAY BROADCAST FROM A SINKING VESSEL. AS THE MAYDAY IS BEING RECEIVED, ANOTHER BROADCAST STEPS ON THE EMERGENCY CALL AND COMPLETELY DISTORTS THE MAYDAY EMERGENCY CALL. AS A RESULT OF THE MAYDAY BROADCAST BEING INTERUPTED, ONLY PARTS OF THE LOCATION OF THE SINKING VESSEL ARE RECEIVED BEFORE COMMUNICATIONS WITH THAT VESSEL ARE CUT OFF. ORDERS ARE IMMEDIATELY DISPATCHED TO U.S. COAST GUARD STATION, GREAT EGG BASE AND U.S. COAST GUARD STATION, CAPE MAY. BOTH BASES RESPONDED. CAPE MAY LAUNCHES A HELICOPTER, GREAT EGG SENDS A 41-FOOT UTILITY BOAT. BOTH TEAMS ARE GIVEN THE BEARING 135 DEGREES, LOCATION 20-25 NAUTICAL MILES OFF OCEAN CITY,

NEW JERSEY. RADIO COMMUNICATIONS ARE SET UP
AS A SEARCH PATTERN IS INITIATED.

(The term 'stepped on' is used when someone is transmitting a radio message and someone else on the same channel tries to transmit another message at the same time. Both messages will be distorted or unreadable.)

* *

I watched as Dwayne dropped the mike, knowing that the radio was also under water, and started moving toward the bow of the boat in chest-deep water. I started toward the front of the boat where everyone else was and noticed a pair of yellow storm pants floating by. I grabbed them and tried to attach them to the outrigger, intending to raise them as a distress flag, but the pulley broke when I tried to raise them up.

I could feel the boat sinking under me and had a hard time believing this was all happening so fast. It was sinking, stern first, and the only visible deck area was all the way forward where Art, Joe, Duffy and now Dwayne were hanging on.

As I pulled myself toward the front of the boat, I noticed they all had life jackets on.

"Where are the life jackets?" I yelled.

All four voices came back at the same time, "In the center console. Hurry up and get one," they yelled.

I turned around and, going as fast as I could, located the center console. We were in blue water, which made it easy to see and locate it. I took a deep breath and lowered my head below the surface of the water. The shock of the water on my face and the silence of being underneath it added to the difficulty of the task in finding the life jackets. I tried to adjust, but I couldn't. I kept looking at the sun's rays that outlined the sinking boat. Panic was setting in and I tried not to look at the blue depths surrounding the sinking boat. I pulled myself down to the cabinet door, which was already open, to find nothing. I had plenty of air left in my lungs as I swam back to the surface.

I hollered, "I couldn't find them!"

Again the yells came back, "They're in the center console!"

With half the preparation of the first dive, I slipped below the surface of the water again and headed for the open door. Fear of the boat rolling over on me started to enter my mind as I felt the boat shift back and forth. I reached the cabinet door and realized the life jackets had to be floating. I reached in and up, putting my arm in all the way to my shoulder. I felt the floating life jackets and grabbed one.

Looking up at the shining surface confused me because of just how fast everything was happening. The fear of the boat rolling over and trapping me was still on my mind. It was hard not to give in to panic.

The boat was sinking faster than anyone would have ever thought it could. I reached the surface with the life jacket in my hand and made my way to the bow. I asked if anyone had grabbed the flare gun. They hadn't. Duffy held my life jacket and gave me a quick explanation as to where it was. I went back again to the sinking end of the boat, dove under and found the gun and flares right where Duffy told me they would be. When I returned, Duffy took the flares and flare gun while I put on my vest.

Art asked if we had gotten the 'May Day' out and if we thought anyone had received it.

Dwayne said, "Yeah. We got it out. I'm sure I heard them respond before the radio went under."

Then Art asked, "Who's got the time?"

I turned to look at Art and got a good look at the lump he had on his forehead. As I gave the lump a closer inspection, I asked if it hurt. He answered that it didn't hurt half as much as losing his glasses. Art wore glasses his whole life and was very dependent on them.

"It's seven-thirty and time to get out of the boat," replied Joe, with unintended humor. He then slipped uncontrollably out of the sinking boat. It no longer served as a safe refuge.

Slipping out of the little bit of the hull that was still floating, we all started to realize how helpless we were. There was nothing under us and nothing to hold onto. All we could do was float in the midst of all the debris from the boat. I think our bodies were acclimated to the water already because there had been no time to think about it.

Once we were all out of the boat, I asked, "Do we have any rope?"

"No, but there's plenty of it in the anchor locker in the bow," Joe said. "I pulled a lot of it out, hoping it would float. It's right there."

I pulled myself over to the bow of the hull, which was now floating about two feet out of the water. I unclipped my life jacket, handed it to Art and went below the surface of the water. Joe was right. There was a large ball of rope just a few feet below the bow. I grabbed it and returned to the group, handing it to Joe. As I put my life jacket back on, I saw Joe trying to untangle the rope. I was getting my pocketknife out when Joe started yelling that he was being pulled down. I hurried to get my knife open as Joe began slipping below the surface.

He started gulping, "What should I do?"

I grabbed the rope I thought was pulling him down and, in two pulls, had it cut in half.

Joe was still in trouble. "It's pulling me down!"

"Let it go!" I hollered, now realizing I must have cut the wrong end.

Before I could help him, he was pulled under. Everyone made an attempt to grab him, but he was just out of reach of all of us. For a fearful few seconds, we all looked at the spot where Joe had been only a split second ago. Then, with no warning and much to our surprise, Joe popped up, almost exploding into the air. We all sighed in relief as Joe started apologizing for letting go of the rope. He had no idea that we were just trying to recover from our fear he had drowned.

As we began to calm down, I thought about how there had been no time to panic about our situation. To be honest, I thought it was incredible that no one had been badly hurt, much less cut and bleeding.

"Who's got a waterproof watch?" I asked.

Joe was the first one to say something funny and his timing couldn't have been any better.

"I do," he said, "But it's only good up to a hundred and fifty feet." It wasn't much of a joke, but it was enough to put us all in the right frame of mind; we were still alive, all of us.

"It's seven forty-five," said Joe.

"Yeah, that's what I got, too," said Duffy. Then he added, "There she goes," as the bow of the hull slipped below the surface of the water with no hesitation. We all watched as the boat disappeared into the blue depths we were floating in. The time span from when the wave hit the boat until it sank was less than twenty-five minutes.

"She was a good boat and a lot of fun," Duffy said, watching the hull until it had completely disappeared. We were all quiet as we watched it disappear.

I know Duffy had no choice but to accept the circumstances of the situation we were in, but I thought it was very noble of him to seem to just let it go like that. It may sound silly to some, but anyone who has ever owned a boat will understand what I'm saying. Most men form a bond with it; that is to say, they like it in a way that is hard to explain. There is a true sadness felt when an owner loses his boat. I guess it would be like living in a house you really like and having a fire suddenly destroy it. There is a real sense of loss and right then I knew Duffy was feeling that loss.

I watched the boat disappear into the blue depths beneath and had my first inkling of fear. It was almost paralyzing. I felt strong and knew I could make it, but there was still that scary feeling of helplessness. Then I started thinking of all the personal things that had just gone down with the boat. My two best fishing poles and my new hat from Montauk. It wasn't until I looked up and saw the faces of the other guys that I realized how shameful and silly a thought it was that had just gone through my mind.

The wind was still blowing in small annoying gusts and Joe mentioned it might not be a bad idea to grab the cooler that was floating a short distance from us. Dwayne left the group and swam over to the open cooler. Instead of coming back to the group, he started inventorying the contents by himself.

"Just bring it over here!" Joe yelled. "It will give us all something to hold onto."

It wasn't much, but when Dwayne returned with the cooler, everyone put one hand on it. It felt good to hold onto something. The cooler turned out to be more than just an object to touch; it calmed us.

"Holy shit!" yelled Duffy, with sudden excitement in his voice.

"What?"

"What is it?"

Question after question filled the air as everyone waited for an explanation from Duffy who was looking down at the water.

"Look around us! All the bait fish!"

It didn't take long for everyone to realize that the three slabs of butterfish bait had come out of the boat when it sank and was now floating all around us. We started to show the first real sign of panic, and it was certainly warranted. Each of us was aware of what could happen with this much bait floating around us. Some of the fish were floating and some were sinking to what seemed to be different depths. There was real concern, but no solution to the problem. Swimming away would only add sound and commotion to the situation, which we all knew would attract sharks.

We were now in a tight circle around the cooler, each trying to get a hold of our thoughts. I mentioned to the others that the fish would float farther and farther away from us and that it should all eventually sink. After about fifteen minutes, you couldn't see any of it. This made everyone feel a little better.

Checking the horizon for boats, we found that it was almost impossible to see anything because of the waves. The fact was that our heads were the only things sticking out of the water. We were floating in between the waves and up the sides, but almost never at the tops of the waves for very long. We did notice that, about every five minutes, the wave pattern would be just right and we would be at the tip of the wave, allowing us to look in all directions. However, this only lasted for a second or two. We came up with the idea that we would all gather around the cooler and stabilize it, then one of us would pull himself up on his arms and look. The waves would lift us up then drop us right back down, so the only chance we had for this to work was those few seconds when we were at the peak of the wave. Whenever we were dropping or down between the waves, the person whose turn it was to look had to judge for himself the best time to push up from the cooler to see.

Duffy, Dwayne and I were the lookouts, mainly because Art had lost his glasses and Joe, after trying it a few times, confessed it was hard for him to balance himself. We were constantly disappointed each time we heard the report 'nothing in sight'.

It had only been about a half-hour since the boat sank and not too much was being said between us.

"How about taking a vote to shoot off a flare?" I offered.

"Sounds like a great idea," Art said.

"Go for it," Duffy chimed in.

We were all hoping the flares still worked after getting so wet.

Everyone was still holding the cooler stable while I opened the plastic bag and pulled out a flare. I was holding it like it was a bar of gold, really concentrating on what I was doing and trying not to drop the flare or the gun. It wasn't as easy as you might think. As I worked with both hands, Art held my life jacket by the shoulder and Joe held my other shoulder. The cooler was like a moving tabletop, rolling with the waves. I grabbed one flare and made sure the other two were as deep into the pockets of my jeans as I could get them. Next, I put both elbows on the cooler, holding the flare gun in one hand and the shell in the other. I opened the flare gun chamber and made an unsuccessful attempt at hitting it with the shell. Next, I tried putting my forearms together on top of the cooler. This worked perfectly; the shell went straight in. I locked the chamber and pulled back the hammer. Even with the sounds of the wind and the waves, the click of the hammer could be heard and everyone sort of stared at the loaded flare gun.

"Here goes!" I said, as I aimed slightly into the wind and up. A loud 'pop' and a brief smell of sulfur followed.

We all watched with our heads up, the flare soared into the air and returned back to the sea – maybe a little faster than we had hoped it would, but at least we knew it worked and we had two more, so things weren't hopeless.

Art, who was still holding my shoulder, said, "I'm sure glad that thing worked!" It wasn't hard to tell that we all were filled with fear, but we kept it to ourselves.

"Man, we're in deep shit if they didn't hear that Mayday," Duffy repeated.

I turned to Duffy. "I know they'll respond to it. I heard them." It was one thing I was positive of and I was not going to let myself be convinced that I didn't hear it. Then I said to him, "What time is it anyway?"

"Twenty minutes to nine," he said.

"There! It hasn't even been an hour. If they're looking, it could take up to four hours to cover the course we took. Let's get a hold of ourselves."

Out of the clear blue sky, Dwayne said, "Boy, I wish I had a cigarette."

Joe answered, "Dwayne, this would be a great time to quit," which brought another needed laugh. Keeping on the bright side, Joe continued, "You know, this is the first time I ever used this waterproof watch. Boy, it works great!"

I said, "I would be going to church right now if I was home. What would you be doing, Art?"

"Taking Joey and Anna out to breakfast and then church. We go at eleven."

"I'd be reading the paper and sipping on a cup of hot coffee - that's what I'd be doing, but out on the porch, on the bay," said Duffy. "How about you, Dwayne?"

"What?" he said.

Duffy repeated, "What would you be doing if you weren't here right now?"

"I don't know," he grumbled. No one pushed it.

* *

COAST GUARD REPORT

AFTER TWO HOURS OF SEARCHING, BOTH THE UTILITY BOAT AND THE HELICOPTER REPORT NEGATIVE RESULTS IN THE INITIAL SEARCH AREA. THE MAYDAY TRANSMISSION IS REPLAYED AND THE ORDERS ARE GIVEN TO EXPAND THE SEARCH AREA AND CONTINUE THE SEARCH.

* *

It was getting harder and harder to keep panic from setting in as we all found our only comfort in holding onto the cooler. Every five minutes or so, we tried our little boat-watch from the top of the cooler. It was now nine-thirty and the sun was well up into the sky. It was coming up on two hours that we had been in the water. Our spirits were getting low with not even a boat sighting. It was hard to find things to talk about, even though we all knew that talking would help the time go by.

Suddenly, we all watched in wonder as Dwayne let go of the cooler and began rolling and jerking in the water, only to stop and raise one of his sneakers up above his head. As we watched in amazement, he threw the sneaker as far as he could.

"What are you doing?" I asked, only to have him ignore my question and go into the same pattern, ending with throwing his other sneaker away. Next, he was wriggling and keeping his hands below the surface of the water. This time he pulled up his pants, which he had taken off and rolled into a ball and was preparing to throw them, too.

I couldn't help myself. "What are you, crazy? What are you doing?"

"They told us in the Coast Guard to get your shoes off and pants, if necessary, in this type of situation."

"Well, I don't care what they taught you in boot camp, there's no reason to do that now and if we hit jellyfish you're gonna cry. What did they tell you to do if sharks are attacking you?" I asked. I then realized I had just said the word everyone had been trying for two hours not to even think about.

Duffy spoke up and supported me, "I'm not taking my pants off. He's right, Dwayne." Without saying a word, Dwayne began to put his pants back on.

The next question came from Joe. "By the way, Dwayne, what did they tell you to do if attacked by sharks?"

"Kick, punch, poke, whatever you can to discourage them."

I ended the questioning by saying that if I had to kick a shark, I would want something between it and my foot.

Duffy spoke up and said, "We really can't talk about sharks. We have to try and not even think about them. Let's have a boat check – it's been awhile. By the way, what time is it?"

"Ten-fifteen. Well, that's almost three hours," I said.

It was Duffy's turn to look and, as I helped steady the cooler, I looked over at Art and said, "Your forehead looks a little better, Art."

"I don't feel it as much as I did earlier. It must not be as bad as I thought."

"Don't believe it; you've got a real goose egg there."

We were now accustomed to the lack of success from our lookout routine, but weren't ready to stop doing it.

When it came around to Duffy's turn again, he said, "I'm not sure, but I think I see something."

"Where?" we all asked.

Duffy was back in the water after his arms gave out waiting for the waves to lift us.

"Let Dwayne look – he's taller."

Duffy again explained what he saw and in what direction. We were filled with new energy and hope as we concentrated on stabilizing the cooler for Dwayne.

"I see it!" he yelled. "It's a sailboat – a big one. It's coming closer. We'll wait to shoot our flares until it gets in front of us."

Everyone was excited and I honestly felt for a minute that the thought of sharks was out of everyone's mind.

"How far off are they? Should we start to swim in their direction?" I asked.

"They're a good five or six miles away," said Dwayne. "All I can see is the sails. But they're going to be passing in front of us."

We had been in the water long enough now to realize that if something didn't happen soon we would have to start swimming in the direction of land because, although the sun was out, the water temperature was starting to lower our body temperatures. We were all starting to look a little pale.

Duffy, Dwayne and I were the only ones who actually got to see the sails on the horizon. Art was upset about losing his glasses, but it was just part of the helplessness we all felt. I moved into position for the next peek at the approaching boat. I waited for what I was sure was the perfect moment. I pulled myself up onto the cooler, looking first in the direction of the sailboat and then gave a quick glance at the horizon.

As I came down to the other guys, I said, "Boy, it's really moving along with this wind. It will probably be in front of us in a few minutes."

We were getting ready to check the location of the sailboat again when a wave lifted all of us up above the surrounding seas, and without the use of the cooler, we all got a good look at the sailboat. Art even said he could make out the sails. The sight of that boat lifted our spirits to the point where no one realized we had been in the water for over three hours.

We began discussing when we thought would be the best time to fire off a flare when Art shouted, "Quiet!"

We all stopped talking and tried to not hear the wind and the waves. One by one, we each started to say, "Yeah! I hear it!" It sounded like a helicopter. We scrunched our eyes and cupped our ears to determine where it was or which way it was coming from and almost forgot about the sailboat until a wave lifted us up far enough to see a small flash of the white sail.

"There! There! It's a Coast Guard helicopter. I see it! I see it!"

I don't really know who saw it first, or if we all saw it at the same time. We were full of joy - for a lot of reasons. We knew now that the Coast Guard had received our Mayday and, on top of that, the search was on. It was starting to look like, in a very short time, we were going to be rescued. The helicopter was close enough now to see the bright orange sign on the side. As we all rejoiced in the water, I checked my pockets for the flare gun and flares.

I pulled the gun up and gave it to Joe and said, "Please, don't drop this."

I reached into my other pocket with one hand and placed my other hand over the top of it, just for safety. I had to hold my breath while doing this because, with both arms down like that, my face went under the water. While I was beneath the surface, pulling the two remaining flares out, I opened my eyes and took a good look at myself in the crystal clear blue water. Once again, I was filled with the fear of sharks. Looking down past my bright yellow legs, past my white sneakers, I watched the sun's rays disappear into a dark blue that went eventually to black. I was so used to the water temperature that when I lifted my head out into the fresh air it was more of a shock.

Pulling my head out of the water, I forgot about my arms not being out and started taking in salt water. I pulled the flares out of my pocket, trying as fast as I could to give them to someone so I could expel some of the water out of my mouth and nose. I was expecting to go into a full-scale coughing attack, but didn't. Instead, I just swallowed the water.

"You alright?" asked Joe.

"Yeah, I'm fine," I said. "I just took in a little water. God, I hope this is it," meaning our rescue.

The helicopter was about a mile away and maybe two hundred feet up. It was obvious that they were searching and everything seemed to be going great. As we watched, the helicopter turned broadside to us. We could only guess that they were looking at the passing sailboat.

Dwayne announced, "I'm going to shoot a flare."

Everyone waited for the 'pop,' but instead, there was just a 'click'. This brought more of a reaction from everyone than sighting the helicopter.

Joe was still holding the two remaining flares. He tried to calm everyone by shouting, "It's okay! It's okay! We forgot to put the new flare in."

There was more than enough time to load, but everyone yelled with excitement to hurry and get the flare off. This uncontrollable excitement had a hold on us all. It seemed like everything was happening just as fast as when the boat sank.

In less than a minute, Dwayne got the gun loaded and held it high in the air. There was a dull 'pop' as our second flare went screaming up over our heads. There was the familiar smell of sulfur as we watched the small red ball reach its highest altitude, then start to return back to the sea about thirty feet away from us.

We waited half a minute without anyone saying a word.

"Shoot another flare," yelled Duffy.

We all supported his idea with our own yells, "Shoot another!"

No one looked at each other as we held the cooler, watching the gun get unloaded and then reloaded. Dwayne fired the third and last flare. It followed the same pattern of flight as the first one.

As soon as I heard the 'pop', I let go of the cooler and swam about six feet away. It was the first time I had left the cooler since we had pulled together on it. I didn't like the feeling of floating, but knew it was the best thing to do. I started yelling as loud as I could and waving my arms in the air. Duffy, Art and Joe did the same. Dwayne stayed with the cooler.

"Here we are! Here! Why the hell aren't you coming?"

Everyone continued to wave and shout, but nothing seemed to change as we watched the helicopter just hover over the sailboat. After about two minutes, the helicopter turned and headed off, away from us. During this time, the sailboat had cruised by us, too. I would say, at its closest point, it was one mile away.

Suddenly we found ourselves upset over what had just happened; the helicopter went off in the wrong direction and we had missed being noticed by the sailboat. Despite our disappointment, our spirits were still good because we knew the Coast Guard was looking for us.

"What time is it?" I asked.

"Ten-thirty."

We all came back to the cooler with mixed feelings of hope and confusion over our near rescue.

"Why didn't they see us?"

"I'll tell you why – they were probably checking the sights out on that sailboat," said Joe.

"No," I moaned. "Turn around and look behind you."

As everyone turned, they realized what I had already figured out. The glare from the sun was blinding and anyone looking in our direction would never see anything. It was early and the sun wasn't high enough yet, making it impossible to look out to sea. At least we knew why, now, and were filled again with the hope that it was just a matter of time before they found us.

"Listen," I said. "I have an idea that will help. We're not doing any good just drifting. How about if we start swimming back in the direction of the Twenty-eight Mile Wreck? We're bound to come across some sport fishing boats. As it is, we're in 'no man's land' here."

"Sounds good," said Art.

Art's support for this idea was comforting to me. I guess that's why we're good friends. Dwayne wasn't talking too much. Joe and Duffy seemed to be okay with the idea of swimming. With the sun in its present location, it was easy to locate the direction we would have to swim in order to reach the Wreck.

As we were preparing to start, I asked, "What's in the cooler?"

With that, the top was pulled off and, bobbing in about six inches of water, there were three sodas and two submarine sandwiches.

"Anybody want to try these sandwiches?" asked Joe.

"No," was the reply all the way around, except for Dwayne. He reached in and pulled out the closest one. Then he ripped the paper off and exposed a waterlogged sandwich that appealed to me about as much as the salt water I had swallowed earlier.

"What are you going to do with that?" Duffy asked him.

"See if there's anything on here I like," was his answer.

I didn't know if Dwayne was joking or not, but he began picking the sandwich apart, bit by bit, and flinging the pieces away from him as he completely demolished it. He didn't even eat any of it. It didn't seem to bother anyone or make anyone laugh, if that's what he was trying to do. But, when he went in the cooler for the other sandwich, I spoke up.

"Dwayne, please don't do that anymore."

"What?" he asked.

"Tear the sandwich up and throw it all over. You're only going to attract fish and possibly sharks."

He stopped.

"How about we all share a soda?" someone suggested, just to get away from the shark subject again.

"What's in there?" asked Joe.

"One orange, one root beer, one coke."

Joe said, "Look, orange is as close to breakfast as you can get. Let's have the orange."

As we all floated around the cooler waiting for the can to get to us, I remember thinking to myself, 'I really don't need this.' But, when I took a sip of the warm orange soda, it tasted so good that all I could do was hope it would come around again – and it did. This time, when the can was placed in my hand, I remember being thankful and glad that there was enough for another sip. The soda really did refresh us. When it was finished, we decided to have another at around lunchtime.

"What time is it?" I asked.

"Ten forty-five."

"If we push, we could be at the Wreck, or near it, in two or three hours," I said. "We'll have another soda then."

* *

COAST GUARD REPORT

WITH LITTLE INFORMATION TO GO ON AND A NEGATIVE RESULT OF THE FIRST SEARCH, TWO C.A.S.P. BUOYS WERE DROPPED INTO THE OCEAN. ONE BUOY WAS PROGRAMMED TO SUPPLY INFORMATION THAT WOULD BE EQUAL TO THE LIKELY DRIFT DIRECTION AND SPEED OF A DISABLED BOAT. THE OTHER BUOY WAS PROGRAMMED TO GIVE INFORMATION THAT WOULD BE EQUAL TO THE LIKELY DRIFT DIRECTION AND SPEED OF A SURVIVOR IN THE

WATER. THIS INFORMATION WOULD BE USED TO SET
UP THE NEXT SEARCH PATTERN.

* *

CHAPTER SEVEN

Everyone agreed and we started swimming in the direction of the Twenty-eight Mile Wreck. At first, we all tried to stay together or near the cooler. We had to swim into the wind, which blew water into our eyes and mouths continuously. Even if you kept your mouth shut, water would get in your nose.

After about fifteen minutes of swimming, it became obvious that we would have to break up and swim as singles. Until this point, we had all tried to stay within arm's length of the cooler. But, if we planned to swim all the way back to the Wreck, we wouldn't be able to do it as a group. I started by pushing off and, I must say, once away from the group, the fear of sharks again entered my mind.

Next to leave the cooler was Art, who came over to about three feet away from me and in a strong but low voice said, "Dave, I can't see that well, so do me a favor and lead."

"Sure, no problem."

It was at that moment that I confided to Art in a low voice, "I wish that bait was still in the bait well. I'm having a hard time keeping the fear of sharks out of my mind."

Art said, "I'm not going to worry about them until they get here."

I laughed and said, "You've got a good approach there."

Next to leave was Joe, with a very serious look on his face. Knowing Joe's sense of humor as well as we did, both Art and I knew that look could change in a second. All he said, though, was, "This really is a lot easier than hanging onto the cooler."

Duffy and Dwayne were both still holding onto it as we swam in the direction of the Wreck. Eventually, we started to separate. It was easy to be the lead with the exception of having to stop every now and then to wait for the other guys to catch up. For some reason, swimming gave me something to do and I found that it helped me to forget about the sharks.

We followed the same pattern for about an hour-and-a-half. It seemed like we were doing pretty well and the sea was calming down a little bit. The wind still blew with annoying gusts that constantly made the salt water burn our eyes and, if we tried to get a breath of air through our mouths, it would cause us to choke. Every other stop I would have to wait for the group to catch up. Then I would ask what time it was.

Joe never seemed to get agitated about my asking. I think he never looked at his watch until someone would ask him, because he always answered like he was surprised himself about how much time had passed.

Our swimming order was - I was in the lead, Art was second, Joe third, and Duffy and Dwayne were both together bringing up the rear on the cooler. As I swam, Art would follow and, if he started swimming to the left or right too much, Joe would yell out which way he would have to swim to get back on track. It would have been easy to become separated, the way the waves were. If I got three waves in front of Art, he lost sight of me and Joe could only see me every other wave. Very rarely did I see Duffy or Dwayne, except for when I would stop and wait for the group to pull together and start all over again.

I have never had a fear of the ocean, but I can honestly say I have always respected it and, as I swam into the on-coming waves, they reminded me of a time when I was in the Navy. It was 1970 and the Vietnam War was going strong. I was stationed on a destroyer escort, the *U.S.S. Garcia* D.E. 1040 out of Newport, Rhode Island. I didn't care much for service life, but I did like being on the ship. I was one of the few who really enjoyed going out to sea.

As I looked at the on-coming waves, swimming over each wave and down the back sides of them, I was reminded of this particular incident back then. We were told we would be heading into a North Atlantic storm and that we would be called to general quarters (battle stations) until we passed through the storm. At first I was excited, thinking nothing could happen to us on this ship. The *Garcia* was about three hundred seventy-five feet long. Its main deck was about thirty-five feet above the water line. On its forward deck was a five-inch gun mount, about twenty-five feet tall, with two missile launchers right behind it. Amidships had two sets of torpedo tubes. On the fantail of the ship was a helicopter pad that housed a small helicopter carrying two missiles. The Garcia was small compared to other ships in the fleet, but I can tell you it hardly ever rocked, even in rough seas.

The storm was six hours away and we were called to a special meeting in the mess hall. It turned out that this storm was much bigger than anyone expected it to be. We were told that we didn't have enough fuel or time to make it back to port, so the plan was to head straight into the storm. Once we were through the storm, a tanker would meet us, we would refuel at sea and then head back to our home port.

Four hours later, the call came for general quarters. My job (which I loved) was port lookout. Even though there were systems, like radar and such, there was always a human lookout in case of electronic failure. Both port and starboard lookouts were called into the bridge. We watched as the seas began to build and the winds increased.

After three hours of heading into the storm, the waves increased to thirty-five feet and then to forty-five feet. I was holding onto a steel beam and watching as the bow of our ship took on wave after wave.

The bow would start to disappear into a wall of blackish-blue water, which would cover the deck, smashing into the gun mount as the entire deck would go under water. The water continued to rise until it completely covered the gun mount. It looked like the ship was sinking, but instead there would be an explosion of white seawater as the ship then erupted out of the sea and rose up so high that all I could see was clouds. Then the ship would start to come down and, as it did, the next wall of blackish-blue water would come into view. And the cycle would begin again.

That was all a long time ago and I thought it would be one of those things I never forgot, but as I swam over each wave, I felt like I was reliving that adventure.

When I thought it was about one o'clock, I stopped swimming and waited for everyone to catch up so we could share another soda and, I mean to tell you, I was really looking forward to that can of soda. As I floated over the never ending waves, I could see Art only two waves away and I yelled to him, "What do you say we stop for a soda?"

"I was really hoping you'd say that!" he yelled back.

I looked for Joe and was relieved when I saw him about six waves back and slightly off course, compared to us, but in no real danger of losing sight of us. I could also see Duffy and Dwayne, who were not much farther behind Joe than they had been for the last hour. I don't think we were ever more than a hundred yards apart. I was now within arm's length of Art and was looking for Joe. Instead, I saw Duffy and Dwayne. Joe had fallen behind them.

I said to Art, "Boy, it looks like Joe is starting to have a hard time."

Just then, I noticed Duffy and Dwayne pointing toward the west. I turned my head in that direction. The wind started burning my eyes, but I could easily see a Coast Guard helicopter cutting across the sky, heading dead East at a high rate of speed. It was traveling too fast to be looking for survivors. Nevertheless, it was still out here. It had to be looking for us.

I tried to explain the helicopter's location to Art, who was straining his eyes to see it. By the time I could explain, it had moved far enough to be in another location. It basically crossed the path we were headed on, which was just what we needed to see to lift our spirits.

Duffy and Dwayne were now hanging back a little for Joe, who was lying on his back and just kicking with his feet. Both Art and I wanted that soda now, so we agreed to just swim back and meet them. They were just a couple of waves behind us. When Duffy and Dwayne met up with us, they looked almost dry with their chests and stomachs on top of the cooler. As I got closer to Joe, I could see that he had lost a lot of his natural color. We all pulled together at the cooler and were full of excitement over spotting the helicopter.

I asked Joe if he had seen it and he said he had. I assured him that it was just a matter of time before they found us. I ended by saying I wished I had another flare.

Joe added, "Look, while you're wishing, why don't you wish for a boat?"

This was a good sign to me because I knew that Joe wasn't really as bad as he looked.

"Oh, well. Let's get down to business. What will it be for lunch guys – Coke or root beer?" I said.

Art answered and said, "I don't care – just open it, will you?" He laughed and added, "I've been dreaming of those sodas."

There was a silence in the air and Duffy mumbled that he and Dwayne drank the sodas earlier.

"You what?" I said, which was almost in harmony with Art.

"I know, I know," said Duffy, who was the spokesman for the two. "There's nothing that can be done about it now. We did it, okay?"

"Well, you're right there," I said. "There's nothing that can be done about it."

"Just drop it," insisted Duffy.

"Fine," I said. "Well, at least they're still looking for us." But no one talked.

It seemed to me there was no sense in staying in a group, now, and we all knew it. Without saying anything, we prepared to separate.

Joe was the first to speak. "Look, you guys go ahead. I just can't kick anymore and I'm slowing you down. If you get help, just send them back for me, okay?"

Before anybody could respond, Dwayne said, "Fine, will do," as he grabbed the life ring from the top of the cooler, put it under his chest, and started to pull away from the group. I was hoping to see a little remorse from Dwayne and Duffy after drinking the sodas. Maybe it was there and I just didn't see it. Neither of the two had a shameful look on their face.

I spoke up and said, "Wait a minute. How about we just take a little rest and see how you feel in say half-an-hour?"

"Look, you saw the helicopter there up in front of us... looking. We've got to get there," Duffy told us.

I made it very clear that I thought splitting up was a bad idea, but could see that Duffy and Dwayne had made up their minds. Duffy and Dwayne turned and started swimming again in the direction of the Wreck. For the first time since I met Duffy, I had some hard feelings building up in me - first the sodas and now this - wanting to leave one of the group behind.

As Art, Joe and I hung onto the cooler, Art said to me, "Dave, if it weren't for the helicopter sighting, I'd say you were right. But, it's getting late and I feel like I could swim home; that's how strong I feel. I really have to try."

The whole time we were talking, Joe was saying, "Please, just leave me here and send help back after you get picked up."

"Art, be careful. Don't fall behind and lose them. I'm staying with Joe."

You never would have known that Art was missing his glasses because he looked me right in the eyes and said with the most convincing voice I have ever heard, "As soon as they pick us up, we'll be back to get you. Take it easy, Joe. It won't be long until we are all home."

When Art let go of the cooler, I yelled as loud as I could to Duffy and Dwayne, who were already a good ways off, to tell them to wait for Art. I didn't want to, but I know my voice carried a certain demand to it because I watched as they both stopped swimming and waited for him.

As Art swam away, he stopped only to turn around and say to me, "You're a good friend."

I returned his compliment by saying, "You're a better one – see you later."

He added, "Take care, Joe," and swam toward Duffy and Dwayne.

"We'll see ya," replied Joe, but then he went into a little speech to me about how he didn't want me to stay and would I please leave while I could still catch up to the other guys.

"If you don't shut up, I'm going to... to... Gee, I don't know what I'm going to do."

"I mean, please. I'll be alright."

"No," I said. "We'll be alright."

I looked at Joe and told him, "I know Art; he's a tough bird. If they get picked up, he'll be back here - and that helicopter was a good sign. What time you got anyway?"

"Two-fifteen."

I turned and watched as the three bobbing swimmers disappeared into the waves.

"I can't believe they drank the sodas."

Joe, who I must say is a lot wiser than me said, "Don't let that eat at you. It's got to be bothering them more than you."

"You're right," I agreed. "So, how are you feeling?"

"I feel fine. It's just that I can't keep up the pace that everyone was keeping."

I remembered how comforting it was holding onto the cooler after the boat went down and how useful it was during our searches for nearby boats. However, I can honestly say that trying to swim with it had turned into a real burden. The cooler wasn't big enough for me and Joe to get on like Duffy and Dwayne. That would have made it a lot easier to move. So, we both held onto a handle and kicked our feet. It was very hard to swim this way because of our life jackets.

"How about if we let the cooler go and just swim on our backs in that direction? If you get tired, let me know, then we can lock arms and just kick our feet. We have to try not to break the surface of the water with our kicking. Okay?

"Okay."

ART

One of the most gut wrenching decisions I have ever had to make and one that would profoundly affect my existence or end it was when I had to choose whether to try to swim off with Duffy and Dwayne or stay with Dave and Joe. I felt strong enough to swim and thought it would increase our chances of survival. But even though we had agreed to separate because Joe was not doing well and couldn't keep up, there was no dilemma about what I really wanted to do. I wanted to be with Dave and Joe, two guys I knew and trusted. Dave and I had been friends and fishing buddies for years, Joe more recently. After the soda incident earlier in the day with Duffy and Dwayne, I no more wanted to be with these two guys and have to depend on them than be in a snake pit. I really hate snakes.

I made my decision and swam off with Duffy and Dwayne, hoping I wouldn't regret it. It was a horrible feeling watching the distance between us increase ever so slowly. Duffy and Dwayne took off like it was a race, but I knew better and paced myself, plus I felt they had stolen energy from the sodas. I kept looking back toward Dave and Joe, trying to keep them in sight as long as possible. I became the guy in the middle, the link trying to keep us together in one group, even though I knew we would eventually be separated. I was constantly trying to keep both pairs in sight, which was no small feat since I am extremely nearsighted and was sans glasses. I was doing a pretty good job of it for what seemed like forever but was probably one to two hours. While we were swimming the wind had gradually picked up along with a one to two foot chop which isn't much if you're in a boat, but it's brutal with only your head out of the water.

And then it happened. I turned to locate Dave and Joe and they had vanished. I panicked. I called out to them numerous times with no response. I did scissor kicks trying to elevate myself for a better view, hoping to see them. Nothing worked, they were just gone, out of view and out of earshot. We were finally separated.

I called ahead to Duffy and Dwayne and asked them to slow down so I could tell them what had happened. Their reaction was pretty much, "Oh well, that was the plan and we gotta keep moving." Not what I wanted to hear, but not surprising either. These two guys were turning out to be real gems. No longer having a choice in the matter, I decided the best thing to do was focus on the here and now...surviving. I sure could have used a sip of SODA at this point.... man was I pissed off about that, but realized anger would be counter-productive, so I put it out of my mind and tried to calm down.

We continued swimming toward land, or so we thought. With no reference points to judge our speed or direction, we had no idea we were in reality drifting farther south and east, away from land. Conversation was minimal during the rest of the afternoon. We were busy just trying to swim and expend as little energy as possible. By this time, the seas had kicked up a little more, so water was constantly in your eyes, ears, nose and mouth. It was also slowing down our 'progress'.

During the course of the afternoon, we could occasionally see and hear the helicopters searching for us, but never close enough for them to see us. That, I have to tell you, was extremely disheartening. We even saw several small ships in the distance, again too far away for any hope of being rescued. Each near miss was another shot in the heart. But we kept going, no talking, no jokes... just swimming and spitting out salt water while dying for a glass of fresh water.

We had been in the water, now, close to eight hours and the fun was just beginning. I hadn't stopped thinking about Dave and Joe, where they were, were they okay, how I should never have let us get separated. Those thoughts weighed heavily in my gut like I'd been kicked by someone and he forgot to take his foot out. I just couldn't shake it. But you will see, as this story unfolds, that all these events are like the links of a chain. If any one of them had happened differently or not at all, the chain would break and we would not have survived.

* *

COAST GUARD REPORT

AFTER RETRIEVING THE C.A.S.P. BUOYS AND COMPILING THE INFORMATION, A NEW AND MORE CONCENTRATED SEARCH PATTERN WAS SET UP. AS OF MID-AFTERNOON, NO SIGN OF SURVIVORS, DEBRIS OR VESSEL HAD BEEN SIGHTED. THE MOST PROBABLE AREA WOULD BE SEARCHED AGAIN AND WOULD CONTINUE UNTIL DARK.

* *

Sometime in the late afternoon, after hours of silence, swimming and dying of thirst, Dwayne started yelling frantically. Something about a marker or a flag ahead of us. As it became clear that he had indeed spotted a lobster pot marker, we became really excited. It was the first thing we had seen all day anywhere near us that wasn't ocean or sky. We started swimming as hard as we could toward it. As we did that, it gradually became obvious that we might not be able to get to it because of the unreal current we were just realizing was out there. Keeping our aim on the flag, we swung around it until we were swimming directly into the current and toward the flag. This is when it really became fun. We weren't more than ten to fifteen yards from that marker, swimming hard and not going anywhere! This was a cruel joke, right?

There was no reason to state the obvious... that we had to get to that marker or wind up drifting off and dying on the way to England. I decided that somehow I was going to be the first one to reach that marker, so I kicked in the after-burners and found energy

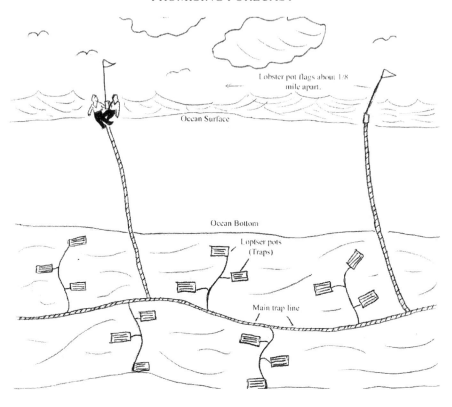

I didn't know was there. At this point, it was every man for himself. There was no way to help someone paddle hard, you just had to do it and we all knew that.

After fifteen minutes of swimming as hard as I ever had to get fifteen yards, I finally was able to reach out and grab that skinny piece of bamboo with a flag attached on top. When I did, the current laid me out on top of the water like a ballyhoo being trolled for marlin. Not a good feeling, I can assure you. I took a second to make sure I had a good grip and then turned to see where Dwayne and Duffy were, huffing and puffing the whole time, trying to catch my breath without inhaling seawater.

Duffy and Dwayne were about five or six yards away and looking like they were fading fast. I yelled to them not to give up and to reach for my hand. I wrapped my feet around the rope going to the bottom and, with my left hand, grabbed the bamboo just above the float. Then I leaned out and reached toward them as far as I could, encouraging them to keep swimming.

Dwayne reached me first and grabbed my hand saying "Don't let go, please." We got a good grip on each other's wrists and I saw that Duffy was right behind Dwayne. I yelled at him to grab Dwayne's leg. A couple more strokes and he did just that. We all took a minute to get our breaths back before trying to make our next move.

There we were: me hanging on to the marker with both feet and one hand; Dwayne, stretched out and holding on to my wrist; while Duffy dangled off the end, hanging on to Dwayne's foot. I'm guessing we looked like a strange form of umbrella rig from underneath. Once we got some oxygen back in our systems, we made our move. Duffy began to carefully climb up the human chain, grabbed the bamboo and wrapped his feet around the descending rope. We both then pulled Dwayne closer and got him situated the same way.

Next, we took the life ring we'd been toting around all day and managed to lift it over the bamboo and stuff the foam marker into the center of the ring. Then we clipped our life vests to the rope that encircled the life ring. We'd been bitchin' about carrying that thing around with us all day and almost ditched it. Thank God, we didn't. Now we were all around the marker, attached to it and in an upright position, able to breathe and relax without sucking in salt water. More importantly, we weren't drifting anymore. Another few links in the chain.

After having to exert ourselves all day, swimming and then sprinting the last fifteen minutes to reach the marker, we were exhausted and it took us a good hour to regain some energy. Then a new problem began to arise. It began with just a few shivers and, over the next hour, developed into total body convulsions. Hypothermia was setting in. Now that we were not exerting ourselves and generating heat, we were cooling off rapidly. Even though the water temperature was in the 68 to 70 degree range, it's still 28 to 30 degrees cooler than the normal body temperature of 98.6. We were getting really cold, really fast. Taking a leak became the most wonderful thing in our little world, just because it warmed us up for a few seconds in between the convulsions.

By this time, it was near 5:00 in the afternoon and one of us noticed what seemed to be a small white freighter heading in our general direction. We watched it for a while, still not talking unless necessary, until we determined that it was going to pass us about a mile away and what we thought was closer to land. By now, the current had slowed down.

We knew that at this distance there was little chance of them seeing us, so we discussed our options, which were limited. Stay on the marker and yell and wave, or leave the marker to swim closer to the freighter and yell and wave. We had no more flares and no signaling devices of any kind. Leaving the haven of our marker was not an easy choice, but we felt we had to take that chance. We had been in the water now over ten hours and didn't know if we could last the night, so off we went, taking our life ring with us and heading for the path the freighter would take.

We swam as hard as we could for maybe a half hour before we had to stop and start yelling and waving. The freighter was now about a half mile away and broadside to us..., as close as it was going to get. We screamed louder and waved harder..., all to no avail. We saw no sign of life on the ship and no indication they had seen us. And they hadn't. We watched forlornly as it steamed off into the distance. Another disappointment and yet another link in the chain.

Now, we all looked at each other trying to figure out 'Plan B'. There we were, bobbing in the Atlantic Ocean without a boat or anything else, except our life ring, somewhere in the neighborhood of twenty-five miles off the East coast, in over one hundred feet of water, with bigger fish than we were also somewhere in the neighborhood. 'Plan B'? I started to laugh harder and harder. I don't know if it was nervous laughter or just my weird English sense of humor, or both, but it did make me feel good and it warmed me up better than the convulsions did. Dwayne and Duffy looked at me like I was crazy..., and just didn't get it. I mean you can't make this shit up. Truth is stranger than fiction.

Shortly after my little outburst, 'Plan B' appeared out of nowhere. Dwayne or Duffy, I'm not sure who spotted... you guessed it... another lobster pot marker. What are the odds?! With very little current now, we struck off for our new goal and reached it rather easily. We positioned our life ring as before and clipped ourselves on and settled in for what promised to be a long night. The chain was getting longer.

While the sun was setting and the wind and ocean were laying down, we could again see and hear helicopters searching for us. It was bittersweet because, although it was encouraging that they were still looking for us, they never came close enough to see and rescue us. They continued to search, even after dark for awhile, and we watched their searchlights glowing in the sky and followed them while they ran their search patterns. Eventually, they called off the search for the night. We were devastated ,yet again. We could only hope that they would return in the morning.

It was somewhere around 8:00 PM now and we were steeling ourselves for a long night in the water. We had already started shivering every few minutes again and now, with the sun down and the air temperature dropping, the water actually felt warmer. We continued to lose body heat and become weaker. The shaking became more violent as our bodies tried to generate heat. The intensity of the thirst I felt was indescribable. My face was sunburned and my lips were cracked yet here we were, surrounded by water we couldn't drink and I'm hooked up with the two snakes who drank the only two sodas we had earlier in the day. God, I wished I had decided to stay with Dave and Joe. I prayed that they were okay... and maybe even rescued already. Little did I know that they were about a half mile away, hooked up to another lobster pot marker. How's that for another link in this ever lengthening chain?

DAVE

It turned out that letting go of the cooler was a good thing. It was no longer a struggle to hold onto it and swim. The freedom of movement made all the difference.

It was working quite well and, as we floated along, we talked about a lot of different things - about when the boat went down, where we thought we were now, even where we thought the other guys were by now.

The ocean was calming down and the wind had slowed to a gentle breeze. It was turning into the day that had been predicted by the weather service. The waves were still high, but spaced far enough apart that it wasn't what you'd call choppy. I began to notice a lot of big ships on the horizon, which did nothing for our hopes of getting rescued because of their distance from us.

As the day went on, the fear of sharks began creeping through my thoughts again. I remembered how we always had luck catching sharks in the morning and late afternoon. I've read that sharks like to eat at night but, from my own experience, I would say they feed whenever food is around. It was now afternoon. The water had lost that storm-gray look and was now clear as ever. I had to keep going back to Art's theory, which was don't worry about them until you have to. As we watched for new tankers to appear, I would occasionally turn and check the horizon all the way around us. The minute I did, Joe would ask if I saw anything.

We found that if we didn't check his watch as much as we had been doing, the time seemed to go by a little faster, which at this point made no real difference. It appeared we had ships in all directions, but not one was within five miles of us. We kept repeating the comforting thought that maybe one would be headed our way and see us, or maybe the Coast Guard had found the other guys and would soon be here for us.

I again checked the horizon and this time I saw something that looked familiar... and within our swimming range. It was a lobster flag... it marked a string of lobster traps! If nothing else, it would be something to hold onto while we waited for help – plus, it was getting late in the afternoon and both Joe and I were getting tired. I made my mind up that we were going to head for the lobster pot flag and tie up to it.

I looked at Joe and said, "We have to get to those flags." They were about two hundred yards to the west.

Joe just said, "Lead the way and I'll follow."

As I turned over on my chest and started to swim as well as I could, I came to realize that the flag I was swimming for was getting farther away. I stopped for a minute to analyze the situation. It was then that I noticed how fast the current was that we were in. If you're floating down a stream, you can tell you're moving just by looking at the shore, but if you're floating and don't have any stationary things to look at, you have no idea that you're even moving. As I watched the flag move away from us, I could see just how fast we were drifting.

Joe was about ten feet behind me and starting to lose his color again, what little he had. I explained the problem to Joe as fast as I could because the next flag, which would be our next target, was in sight and we had no time to lose if we wanted to tie up to it. I changed the direction we were swimming in to one I thought would put us in front of the next flag, thinking we would then drift by close enough to grab it without expending a lot of energy. As we started out, I kept talking to Joe and explaining the importance of getting to the flag. I could see the flag coming closer and realized that there was no way we could make it, even if Joe was up to swimming his best.

"Just keep swimming, Joe, and pray that there's another flag on this string." We were in just about the right position to catch the next flag and I spotted it.

"I can't believe we're drifting this fast. I wonder if it's been like this all day. I'm going to get a hold of it, Joe, and when you see it coming, you swim in that direction and I'll grab you."

Joe looked at me and said, "Dave, I hate to be a pain in the ass, but I just can't swim anymore."

It was then that I got serious with Joe. "If we don't get this flag and it's the last one, we'll have to drift until they find us. That's why we are seeing all the tankers; we're drifting down by the mouth of the Delaware Bay. Put everything you've got into it. I'm going to go tie up. Keep an eye on me and swim as hard as you can."

"Dave, I'll try, but I'm not kidding. I just don't have it in me."

"Do your best. I mean it, Joe. This is important."

As I started to swim toward the flag, I noticed that all I had to do was swim to the left or to the right. The current was moving me faster than I could swim. I could see that I was not going to have trouble grabbing the bamboo pole. As I approached it, I positioned myself perfectly and was now just a few feet away. I reached out and grabbed it, feeling a sense of security, but that changed to fear within a few seconds as I tightened my grip on the bamboo. I felt pressure push against me and, still holding on tight, felt the water wrap over my shoulder and pull me under the surface. It was the first time in a while that my head had been under water and it chilled my whole body. I was filled with panic. I felt the bamboo slipping through my fingers. Still under water, I had to quickly go hand over hand until I had the flag in my hand and I could get my head out of the water. I don't think there was eighteen inches of bamboo left when I was able to position myself where I could keep the water from ripping me away from the pole.

I looked for Joe, who was now kicking and about to reach me.

I yelled, "Try to catch up!" I was afraid of going under again and with the thought that this might be the last flag in the string of pots, I tried to make what I was doing work.

Joe was on his back and the only thing he could do was kick his feet in the direction of my voice. He wasn't looking like he was going to make it. I had water wrapping around my head and causing rapids to form over my shoulder. All I could do to help Joe was yell and stick out my leg in the hope of his hitting it as he passed - which is exactly what happened. As he bumped into my leg, I let go with one hand and grabbed Joe's life jacket at the back of his neck. Suddenly, the rapids formed on Joe's shoulders and all we could do was just lay on the surface of the water and try not to move too much.

I didn't realize how tired I was until I had to hold onto the bamboo pole with one hand, with my arm over my head and behind me, and with the other arm holding onto Joe's life jacket. It seemed like a hopeless idea after five minutes and I was starting to think we would get swept off the pole. I soon realized, however, that if I put my feet in Joe's armpits I could take turns with my arms holding onto the bamboo. All I could think about now was how long we would be able to hold onto the flag and if this strong current was going to keep up.

The bamboo marker, the only stable thing we had to cling to, was one of many markers put out by lobster boats to mark not only the location of the pots, but also the section of the trap line where they would pull the traps up. It was really hard to hold onto the bamboo, but it felt good to have something that was stationary attached to us.

While laying there with the water running over us, I began to think of ways we might be able to move up the bamboo to the base, which was nothing more than a chunk of Styrofoam with a piece of pipe that the bamboo went through. The pipe was just for weight, to keep the flag and bamboo up straight in the water, but it was also where the rope that attached to the lobster pots started. If we could get to that, we could tie ourselves up to it without having to hold on. Then we could just wait for our rescue to come, instead of drifting farther away from them.

From where I was, Joe looked to be resting and the only time he actually moved was when I told him I would be changing hands. He would make sure to hold my feet against his sides by locking hands and pressing his elbows against my feet.

It was hard to hear anything because of the water going over our shoulders, so communication was tough. But the plan was simple – Joe would just roll over and start to pull his way up, with me helping him along with my free hand. Then, once next to me, we would both just pull our way until we were at the base. If it worked, we could tie ourselves to the rope. If it didn't, we would just go back to the end of the bamboo and stay there. We really had nothing to lose by trying.

I prepared to get ready for the move, going through in my mind what I would do and how I would do it. I signaled to Joe and felt his arms wrap around my legs. Once he had a grip, he moved up past me faster than I ever thought he could go. After he passed me, I lost all my stability and I rolled over, which exposed my face to the rushing water.

For some reason, it almost hurt to have my face get wet. It was the only part of my body that would dry off and, even though it really didn't dry, it somehow felt dry. I had a chance to think about it, after a while, and realized that our faces were pretty sunburned.

When we finally made it to the base of the marker, it was obvious to me that bamboo was stronger than I had thought. It had resisted snapping the whole time we were struggling on it against the strong current. I guess being in the water kept it flexible.

I don't know if the currents had actually let up some or if having the two of us on the bamboo made a difference. Not only were we able to get to the base of the marker, but once there, the current didn't seem as bad as it did holding on at arm's length at the end of the bamboo. We looked for excess rope on the line, but there was none.

Joe said, "Let's put our belts around the rope." This worked perfectly.

We positioned ourselves so that one of us was looking in one direction and the other person looked in the opposite direction. That way, we could see in all directions. My right side was next to his right side and, although we could feel the ocean currents wrapping around us, we seemed to be able to stay in an upright position, the way a life jacket would normally float you.

We were now spotting tankers and freighters all around us. One even came close enough that we could see the white water from his wake. We tried yelling for help at the ship, but when we realized we couldn't even hear his engines, we figured we'd better save our strength.

"I wonder how the other guys are?" I asked, just to start up some conversation.

Joe liked talking as much as I did and we both needed to keep our minds busy.

"Oh, God, I hope they're okay. I was just thinking how tired I am and we didn't even swim all afternoon like they did."

After a few minutes of talk like that, we both changed the subject and tried to keep the conversation off negative thoughts. It was hard to do.

I asked Joe what time it was getting to be and his reply was "Five-fifteen."

"How many hours have we been in the water?"

Jokingly, Joe answered, "What do you think I am – a mathematician or something? Only kidding." He laughed, "Old banker's joke. Nine hours and forty-five minutes."

It was at this point we came to the conclusion that this was not only a good place to be, meaning on the lobster pot flag, but this was the most comfortable we'd been all day, if you could say that. It just felt good not to be floating in the ocean unattached to anything. I was tired and I know Joe was. I kept feeling frustrated with myself over the fact that there was nothing I could do to improve or change our situation. The feeling of being totally helpless is an exhausting feeling.

While we were floating there, I started thinking about when the boat went down and if there was anything that could have been done to stop the boat from sinking.

I said out loud to Joe, "I wonder if I had tried starting the motors in gear if there would have been sufficient power to push the boat enough so that the water would have surged out the back of the boat."

Joe said, "If the motors are anything like mine, they wouldn't have even cranked over in gear. They have a safety switch which prevents you from starting in gear. Why?"

"I was just wondering if we could have kept the boat from sinking."

"It did go down quick," Joe added.

Another half-hour went by and the sun started to give the appearance of a late afternoon sky. The wind had really died down and the sea was just large rolls of waves. It really was getting nice, but the early morning conditions had exhausted us and it was hard to feel anything but weak.

Floating next to each other, every now and then one of us would kick the other by accident. This would cause an immediate blast of fear and would only be relieved by the apology or the confession made by Joe or me, whoever delivered the kick. Sometimes we didn't realize we kicked the other guy and would have to ask, "Did you kick me?" The fear was enough to make me stick my head below the surface and scan the area around us. The visibility was good but the blue water, once lit up with the sun's rays, now started to look black. Looking around underwater, I could see my yellow storm gear pants and feet. I knew that if a shark was circling us I'd be able to spot him. I also knew that, in a lot of cases, a shark will come up and bump someone before it attacks.

If I was going to be attacked, I wanted to at least try to discourage him. I still had my pocketknife with me and, after one of my underwater searches, pulled it out of my pocket and said to Joe, "If we get attacked by a shark, I have this knife. How about if I put it here in the Styrofoam and if you or I need it, just go for it?"

Joe laughed and said, "What do you expect to do with that? Piss him off?"

I was a little upset with Joe's attitude because I still felt strong enough to believe that I could fight off a shark and Joe seemed to think it was just hopeless.

I answered him, "Look... it's all we have and I wanted you to know where it was if you needed it."

"Thanks, anyway," said Joe.

By now, there were still about two hours of daylight left and neither one of us talked about the on-coming darkness. I was looking in the direction of land when I thought I saw something. My eyes hurt and I knew they couldn't be trusted after all the salt water and sun glare they had been subjected to. Nevertheless, I concentrated on the object on the horizon and asked Joe to turn around and help me check it out. I explained to him where I was looking and, before I could finish explaining, he yelled out, "I see it! It looks like a plane or a helicopter."

It was much too far away to tell what it really was and, in just a few minutes, it disappeared. This wasn't much, but it was the first real encouragement we had in hours and it felt good just to know that it could be them looking for us again. Joe undid his belt and turned around so he could look in the same direction as me. We watched with hope for another fifteen minutes in the same direction where the plane or helicopter had disappeared. Our efforts were rewarded as a small speck in the sky started to get bigger and bigger. This time it was a little closer and easy to see that it definitely was a helicopter. It was also low enough and slow enough to give the impression that it was searching for something.

As we watched the search, right in front of us, the helicopter would come out of the left horizon and travel to the right. Then it would move a little closer and return to the left and disappear for about fifteen minutes, only to return again a little closer to us. It repeated the sweeping search, coming closer every time it turned. We were overcome with joy, not only for the thoughts that we would be rescued in just a couple more sweeps, but that it meant the other guys must have made it. We had no trouble filling the time spans in between with talk. We even talked about what we were going to have for dinner and how thankful we were that this was all going to be over soon.

It was about six-thirty and the helicopter was just coming into sight from the horizon. This time it was close enough that we could easily see the orange markings of the Coast Guard and we could see the identification numbers on the side. The sun was no longer a factor in spotting us because, where they were looking, they had to look away from the sun. It was easy to surmise that if they didn't see us this time they would certainly see us on the next pass. According to past schedules, it would only be about fifteen or twenty minutes now. That didn't seem like a problem after spending all day in the water.

Watching the helicopter turn and come a little closer, we waved our arms and yelled, but they didn't seem to see us. We were really excited now and didn't want to wait another fifteen minutes, but were starting to think we might have to. Their next pass would be right over us. We watched the helicopter move away from us, then we were suddenly filled with confusion. Right in front of us, it turned toward land and started to head in at a much faster speed than it had been traveling. With anger and disbelief, we yelled and waved our arms, even after it was apparent that they were not coming back.

* *

COAST GUARD REPORT

AFTER SEARCHING ALL DAY FOR THE MISSING VESSEL AND SURVIVORS BASED ON A SEARCH PATTERN SET UP FROM THE INFORMATION OBTAINED FROM THE C.A.S.P. BUOYS, THERE HAD BEEN NO SIGHTING OF DEBRIS OR SURVIVORS AND NO ADDED INFORMATION HAVING COME IN FROM ANY MARINAS WITH REGARD TO ANY OVER-DUE VESSELS, AT SUNSET THE SEARCH WAS CALLED OFF AND THE HELICOPTER AND UTILITY BOAT WERE ORDERED BACK TO THE BASE.

* *

My joy had turned to anger and frustration. How could they get this close and just leave? All I could do was curse the helicopter that I had just praised. It wasn't fair. I just couldn't believe it. It made our present situation seem a little closer to being impossible to cope with.

Joe could see I was having a very hard time calming down. Again, I have to say I really admire his ability to stay cool and collected.

"Boy, talk about shitty days," he said.

When you take into account the lack of sleep the night before and then the day's events up to this point, it becomes hard to control your thoughts. Add to that the frustration of seeing the helicopter give up its search right in front of us and I started to see no point in wasting my strength on emotions that couldn't change a thing. Having our hopes picked up like that and so quickly let down again took its toll.

Being in the water all day was starting to get to me and I said to Joe, "I can't believe they drank those sodas."

Joe, who really was much wiser, turned to me, looked me in the eye and said, "Look, you've got to let that go and concentrate on what's ahead of us, not what's behind us. We're just going to have to gut it out. It looks like we're going to be out here all night and the sooner we accept it, the sooner we can deal with it. Right?"

"You're right," I said, then laughed to show Joe that I had calmed down.

With that, Joe said, "Look, aside from being water-logged, we're all right. We're going to have to make it until morning when they start the search up again."

"That should be at about five," I said. "Plus another half hour to get out here. We'll say six, okay? It's seven o'clock now. That's eleven hours more. I really feel good enough to make it. How about you?"

"I'm fine," he said.

"I'm really sorry I lost it there."

CHAPTER EIGHT

The sun was starting to really sink on the horizon and the water seemed to be turning to a darker blue. If it wasn't for Joe and his ability to calm me down when needed, I think I would have lost my mind. I have never experienced total helplessness before. I have always been able to do something to improve my situation. Not so tonight. It was maddening to dwell on it, so I began to pray for help.

The weightlessness you feel when you're in the water had almost started to feel normal to me. The only problem was that, every now and then, a wave would smack against my cheek or face and I had to swallow a shot of salt water, which I never got used to. It still tasted very salty.

It was starting to get dark fast and, on the horizon, we could see ships with their running lights on. It was not much help to us, but at least it was something to look at as they appeared and disappeared on the horizon.

"I never realized how good that sun felt until it went down," I said to Joe. I was starting to feel the effects of being in the sixty-eight degree water. I waited for what I thought was an hour and asked Joe what time it was.

"Twenty after seven."

"Boy, this is going to be a long night."

"You're right," said Joe. "How would you like to hear my life story? Or, would you like to go first and tell me yours?"

I laughed and said, "You go first, in case we get rescued, I want to make sure I hear yours first."

"Well, maybe you're right," he said. "I don't think I can finish by seven o'clock tomorrow, so how about if I just tell you about my kids?"

Without waiting for my approval, Joe went right into telling me about his family, from the youngest to the oldest - then I did the same. Whenever he got tired, I would take over. It was good to talk about our families. What was really nice was we both were listening to each other, not just being polite.

The night air was cold and around my neck I could feel the water as the air would hit my wet skin and send chills to the tips of my fingers, which were under water. At the time, I didn't realize how badly burned our faces were from being exposed to the sun all day. I'm sure this added to the cold we felt. Time seemed to be passing at an extremely slow pace. I tried to think about everything except time, because it seemed to go by a little faster if I kept it out of my mind.

It was about eight o'clock and the only comfort we had, aside from each other's company, was that about every ten minutes or so we would urinate. With the storm gear on, this made us feel a little warmer for about a minute, then the fluid would cool to the water's temperature.

The sky was absolutely beautiful and, although Joe and I thought we could talk all night, it was getting harder and harder to find and maintain a subject. I remember losing my thoughts while talking about a camping trip and having to just give up on completing the story.

It was nine-fifteen and a full moon had come out. It made the night even more spectacular. Whenever I wanted to, I could look over at Joe and see his face, even the drops of water rolling down his face would shine from the moon's brightness.

I was trying to think of the coldest I had ever been in my life and finally decided on a day when I was deer hunting. It was six below zero and I hadn't dressed properly. I thought about how cold I was that day in the hope of getting my mind off how cold I was right now. All these little head games would work until I asked Joe to look at his watch. I can honestly say that not once was I ever happy to hear the time; it was as if it was standing still.

I remember asking Joe what time it was at ten o'clock. I started to calculate in my head the amount of time before the sun would come up and, when the number eight came up, I knew in my heart that we would never make it another eight. Just the three hours from seven to ten o'clock were like a lifetime. If the sun were out, it would be a different story.

ART

From the moment our boat sank early that morning, we had been consumed with survival. Every move we made and every action we took was a reaction to the situation we found ourselves in, from firing the flares and creating a debris slick, to trying to swim toward boat traffic, to eventually finding ourselves strapped to this second lobster pot marker. We had no time to think of anything else. Oh, I had thoughts of my wife, son and parents, Dave and Joe, and a host of others. Those thoughts were in the background, always there but not dwelled on because we had to focus on taking action to survive or there would be no future for us, other than a watery grave.

Now that we were set for the night, all comfy and hooked up to our marker, it became crystal clear to me that this was it. I was here for the duration. Either someone found me or they didn't. Either I would be alive or I wouldn't. I was totally helpless and at the mercy of God and the elements. They say your life flashes before your eyes before you die. This was very different because there was no urgency. Hell, I had all night or whatever to die, so it was more like slow motion with replay. I could let my thoughts wander and dwell on whatever events and people in my life that I wanted to and think about them as long as I wanted to. This was the life-changing part of this experience for me, these next four to five hours, when I was facing almost certain death, when I was forced to look back at my life and hope I had no regrets, or had left anything undone.

My first thoughts were of my wife and son, my parents and sister and my extended family and friends. I was going to miss all of them. I hoped they would feel the same way. I revisited an idea I already knew, but didn't realize the enormity of it until now. The most precious things in life aren't things. They are people, feelings, experiences, my son's robust laughter, my wife's love....you get the picture. We all know this, but I think we fail to appreciate the depth of its true meaning until we're forced to.

As it became darker, a beautiful, brilliant, full moon began to rise, its reflection sparkling on the sea like diamonds. Stars appeared that I had never seen before and the wind went to sleep, leaving the ocean as smooth as black glass. It was easily the most beautiful night I had ever spent on the water. If only we had a boat to enjoy it from.

It was eerily quiet, save for the occasional whale blowing in the not too far distance. Way out on the horizon, we watched an endless parade of lights traveling north and south, ships lit up from bow to stern, carrying their cargo up and down the East coast. None of them were even remotely heading in our direction. It was at this moment that I realized how alone, how helpless and how insignificant we were in the grand scheme of things. I knew deep in my soul that tonight would probably be my last on earth.

As this realization settled over me, a very strange thing happened. Instead of feeling scared or panicking, a calm came over me like none I had ever experienced. Now, I could think about the important people and events in my life without the distraction of trying to survive. Oh, I wasn't giving up. I just wasn't going to waste what little time I had left trying to change the inevitable outcome. I would much rather revisit as many of the really important feelings and experiences that I could before the curtain fell.

While still watching the freighters parade up and down the horizon, I thought about the first time I ever saw my beautiful wife Anna. Our eyes met across a college campus courtyard. I knew she was special the moment I laid eyes on her. Her beautiful smile and big brown eyes drew me in like nectar does a bee. Years later, she confessed that at that same moment she was thinking, "There goes the guy I'm going to marry someday. He just doesn't know it yet."

We spent many hours that summer, sitting by the lake and talking about everything and anything. We shared stories about our families, growing up, our likes and dislikes. Anything was fair game. I think that summer we laid a foundation for the rest of our relationship in that we could talk about anything. We became best friends first.

I went back to school that fall and we stayed in touch by letter and phone. As time went on, I realized what Anna already knew. We were in love and it was the real deal. We even survived a six-week cross-country camping trip, living out of a tent and the back of an old 1967 International Travel-all with our trusty Springer Spaniel, Little Dog, by our side. We trekked from New Jersey to Miami to New Orleans, New Mexico, the Grand Canyon, through Arizona, into Los Angeles and on up to San Francisco and the Sonoma and Napa Valley's before getting low on money and scooting home. We camped out in the Chesapeake Bay watershed, the Blue Ridge Mountains, Kaibab National Forest, the Grand Canyon, Big Sur and truck stops. We camped just outside New Orleans, suffering the mother of all heat and humidity; it rained inside the tent and it was next to a railroad yard with boxcars coupling and uncoupling all night long. Sleep ? Not a chance.

I figured that if she could handle all the ups and downs during this relationship boot camp we called a trip for six weeks and still love me then she was worth keeping around. Thank God, she felt the same way.

We even broke down outside Tombstone, Arizona, and

survived that. While cruising westward along the interstate, my trusty Travel-all overheated. The radiator had clogged up from age and just refused to do its job. We limped into Tombstone, adding water every few miles until we found a seedy motel in a questionable part of town where all the buildings were one story adobe construction and 'saloon-door-hanging-on-a-broken-rusty-hinge' run down. Remember, we were on a budget.

I found a radiator repair shop in the phone book and took the truck there the next morning, fully expecting to be ripped off. As we pulled up to this run down, 'junk-all-over-the- place' repair shop, an older tattooed, grizzly-looking guy with a smirk on his face was giving us the stink-eye. 'Okay,' I thought, 'Here we go.'

As I got out of the steaming truck and started to explain our situation, he just put up his hand and said, "Son, I've been where you're at. You're not from around here, are you?" I guess the New Jersey plates were a dead giveaway.

" No sir." I said.

He took a look under the hood and proceeded to give us a long dissertation on radiator removal, dismemberment, cleaning, repair, reassembly and installation. Dollar signs are flashing in front of my eyes and I'm thinking this is the end of our trip.

With the same smirk on his face, he said, "Son, the bad news is I'm gonna have to charge you thirty dollars to fix this thing, and... it's gonna take a couple of hours." As I was picking my jaw off the pavement, he smiled and said, "Have a safe trip and make some memories."

Still marveling at this gentleman's kindness to two strangers, my body went into convulsions again and I snapped back to my reality of helplessness, thirst and cold. Nothing had changed. Freighters were still traversing the horizon no closer than before. The moon, stars and sea were still beautiful, but impartial to our plight.

My son ,Joe, was only twenty-one months old. A baby, an infant... one soon to be without a father. I couldn't stop the tears flowing down my face at this thought. He and I would never get to know each other. I'd never hold him again or hear him laugh. Never play catch with him. Never take him fishing. Never see him grow up into a man and raise his own family. And he would have to do it all without a dad. I can't explain the depth of the sorrow I felt at the thought.

With tears still streaming down my face, I thought about how Anna would suddenly become a single mom and would have to struggle to deal with such life-changing events... and do it without her best friend. We had just bought our first home, had our first child and now she was going to lose me. I felt a strong wave of guilt wash over me, like the wave that washed over the *Hot Stuff* this morning, and wished I had taken up a less dangerous pastime.

My thoughts drifted to wondering how my parents were going to handle this loss. Thinking how I would feel if something had happened to my son gave me a pretty good indication. A deep and hollow feeling overcame me, like someone had just scooped out my soul and there was nothing left but a shell. That they would have to experience this feeling just wasn't fair. Children aren't supposed to die before their parents. Yet it happens all too frequently, every day, all around the world. My heart ached for all those parents, even as it ached for mine.

Thinking about my parents, I began to recall my early childhood. I was born in Jamaica, Queens, New York, but my first memories are of living in Glen Burnie, Maryland. They are few, but very vivid. One was of my first spanking for disappearing from our fenced-in backyard with my buddies. Mind you, I was only three and a half. My parents finally found me and my cohorts not too far away, but down a hillside, playing in a small stream. Thank God, I had a snowsuit on or my cheeks would still be red. That's when I figured out they really loved me. They proved that many times over the years.

My sister, Carol, was born there and we always teased her about being born south of the Mason-Dixon Line and being the only rebel in the whole family. She was outdoors in her carriage, one day, with a mosquito net over her... getting some fresh air. Mothers did that in those days and we got lots of fresh air. My job was to keep an eye on her, being her big brother and all, so I parked my Tonka truck and went over to check on her. My eyes about popped out of my head when I saw this huge spider climbing inside the netting. I screamed for Mom. It must have sounded serious because she was there in a flash. It turned out to be a black widow, although I swore it was a tarantula. I was a hero for a day and was so proud I had performed my big brother duties. To this day, Carol is petrified of spiders and, of course, always has close encounters with them.

As another round of convulsions ground down to a halt, I thought about a recurring dream that I had as a child and how ironic it seemed now. I was about four years old and every night for three months I would wake up terrified, screaming that 'Joon' was going to get me. My mother would have to come to my room and comfort me until I fell asleep again. I vividly remember having these nightmares to this day. The funny thing was that I could never describe what or who 'Joon' was because I never saw this creature in my dreams, but I could feel his presence. I always woke up just before this thing got me and the dream was the same every night until the very last one.

It began like all the others. I sensed myself being hunted by this thing and was running for my life when I suddenly found myself cornered and confronted with the choice of running out to the end of a long wooden pier and jumping into the water (and the unknown), or turning around and letting this thing determine my fate. As an adult, I've always had a slight problem with authority. I guess it started then because I took the plunge off that pier, into the water, never to be hunted by 'Joon' again, and have felt safe in that element ever since... until now.

This is getting old really fast, I thought, as another peeing session warmed me up for thirty seconds. I can't believe none of those ships on the horizon are heading toward shore or us. It was really aggravating and frustrating knowing that help was within view, but with no way of contacting them. We were invisible to them. There was no sense stressing over that, so I continued on my way, daydreaming.

Where was I? Oh yeah, my dad had gotten a job in aviation, his passion, as an air traffic controller at Kennedy International Airport, so we moved back to Howard Beach in Queens, New York. It was here I went on my first fishing trip, on a pier in Jamaica Bay, when the porgies were running. It was fast and furious action with porgies flopping all over the pier and everybody having a good old time. More importantly, I realized, was that my parents had taken the time to not only take me along, but showed me how to bait a hook, hold a pole and reel in a fish. Little did they know what they had started.

Both my parents were fishermen but, to be truthful, my mom and her mom were die-hard, hard-core fisherwomen. Not the kind that have all the tackle and gizmos etc. or have to catch the biggest fish, but the ones that will hang a line out anywhere, anytime, for as long as they could, whether they are catching anything or not. They had fun just being out on, in or next to the water with a pole, crab trap or clam rake in their hands. Some of that had definitely rubbed off on me.

My mother grew up with her parents in a small house with a dock on a canal just off Jamaica Bay. They had a rowboat that they used to go fishing with. They couldn't afford an outboard, so the only way to get out on the bay was to row. The amazing thing to me was that it was no big deal to them.

My grandmother and her sister decided to go fishing one day while my grandfather was at work. So off they rowed to one of their favorite spots and fished all day without catching anything. When it was time to leave and she was pulling her line in for the last time, she felt a lot of weight that shouldn't have been there. Thinking she had a ton of seaweed on her tackle, she swore and kept reeling. When it reached the surface and she saw a five pound lobster staring at her, she screamed and, of course, the lobster let go. Neither one wanted to leave, even though they were late, so they stayed another two hours trying to catch that damn thing and had to row home in the dark , without the lobster, and face the music from Grandpa. That's die-hard.

ﻭﻭﻭﻭﻭﻭ

As I pondered these thoughts, Dwayne began to cry out, "I don't want to die. I don't want to die." Then his face fell forward into the water. I pulled his head up and said," We're gonna be okay, Dwayne. Just relax, it's okay." That seemed to calm him down and things got quiet again. He was half out of it, so Duffy and I kept an eye on him to keep him from drowning on us.

Off in the distance, we heard another whale blowing as we went into yet another round of convulsions. I couldn't wait to pee again.

* *

COAST GUARD REPORT

9:30 P.M., RECEIVED PHONE CALL FROM MRS. BARBARA JONES ASKING IF ANY BOATS HAD CALLED IN BROKEN DOWN OR WERE BEING TOWED IN. INFORMED HER THAT THERE WERE NO REPORTS OF BREAK-DOWNS OR BOATS IN TOW, BUT THAT WE HAD RECEIVED A MAYDAY CALL AT 7:17. INSTRUCTED HER TO CHECK MARINA WHERE THE BOAT WAS DOCKED.

9:55 P.M., RECEIVED PHONE CALL FROM MR. FRED PAULDING REPORTING THE BOAT MISSING. WE INFORMED HIM OF OUR SEARCH EFFORTS. CONTACTED THE THIRD DISTRICT TELECOMMUNICATIONS CENTER AND INFORMED THEM OF THE MISSING VESSEL.

* *

When my father was offered a job opportunity at the Federal Aviation Administration Technical Center in South Jersey, he jumped at the chance and we moved down to Northfield. It was the best thing he could have done for our family, especially us kids. It was a wonderful place to grow up. My dad being a fisherman, too, immediately found and joined the Atlantic City Saltwater Spinning Club, a group of gnarly old local surfcasters who fished beaches all over the area, all year long. He would often let me tag along on trips and tournaments.

I remember fishing many times on the north end of Brigantine and catching kingfish, blues, stripers etc. I always looked forward to those trips and sadly thought that there would not be a chance for me to thank my dad again and tell him how much they meant to me.

As I finished that thought, something bumped into my leg... and it wasn't Dwayne or Duffy. Adrenalin pulsed through my body as I prayed that it wasn't a shark checking me out for dinner. Those cartilaginous bastards would eat anything. I suddenly wasn't cold anymore as I pulled in my legs and curled up my body as tightly as possible and just waited, praying that it was only a submerged log or other debris drifting by. It was impossible to see down into the glassy black water and, with the full moon above, I have never felt lower on the food chain than right then. All I could do was wait and pray.

Minutes passed by without incident, my body began to uncurl from the fetal position and the adrenalin faded. Then the convulsions began again and I felt colder than I thought was possible. As I gazed out to the ships on the horizon again, I couldn't shake the feeling that something had changed. I couldn't put my finger on it and was too tired to try and figure it out, so I just let my mind wander again.

When I was about twelve, my dad decided it was time to buy a boat for the family fishing excursions. He found a used (beat to crap) 1963 Boston Whaler hull and bought a new trailer and 65hp Mercury outboard for it. We scraped, sanded, patched and painted this boat until it was respectable. Since Whalers are unsinkable, we just had to make it look good... and we did.

A whole new world opened up for us as we began to explore all the back bays, from Ocean City, north to Great Bay. Fishing became even more exciting and productive. Now, we had mobility. It didn't hurt that we also now had a vessel to water ski off of, too. In high school, myself and three friends would load up the boat with gas, food and skis, travel up Patcong Creek to the Cove, unload all the extra stuff and ski all day long. Then we'd travel all the way home, exhausted, making it home just before dark. Man, it was good to be young.

Memories of endless summer days of fishing, crabbing, clamming and waterskiing coursed through my mind as I stared at the lights on the horizon. Nothing seemed to have changed when suddenly it dawned on me that something was different about one set of lights. It wasn't moving north or south and appeared to be motionless... and it wasn't shaped like the rest of the lights. Instead of being long and drawn out, it was short and pointy, like a Christmas tree.

I wasn't sure if this meant anything, but decided to mention it to Duffy and see what he thought. He glanced up and pretty much blew me off saying , "Nothing has changed. It's probably just a sailboat." He's probably right, I thought, as I continued to watch this new set of lights. For a second, I thought it looked a little bigger and a little closer. "Nah," I thought. "I'm just really tired and I can't see shit without my glasses anyway."

Then the shakes hit again. They seemed to be getting more violent and didn't seem to be warming me up much. I wondered if losing consciousness wasn't too far off. I wasn't urinating as often either. After peeing all day, with no fluid going in, I wondered how much could be left. Kidney failure came to mind. Those two purloined sodas we never got to share were becoming more important as time went on. And here I am with the two rat bastards that drank them. I wanted to drown them right there, but I didn't have the energy. I started to shake again. The convulsions were getting closer and closer together as the night wore on and I was getting colder and weaker and thirstier, if that was possible.

I wanted to smack myself for getting so negative. I decided to set the goal of staying conscious, at least until morning. The owner of these lobster pots had to come check them at some point. I just hoped we were still alive when he did. If not, at least our families would have some closure and be able to say goodbye to us. At this last thought, I felt like crying, but there were no tears left. I hoped Dave and Joe were faring better than we were.

I looked up at the brilliant moon and the thousands of stars as they reflected off the ocean and wondered how I could think it was such a beautiful night at the same time I was getting closer to death. Shouldn't I be pissed off and angry at God for ignoring our plight? I didn't have an answer for that and didn't have time to come up with one because, as I looked at the horizon again, I suddenly realized that those lights that looked like a Christmas tree were getting larger. It slowly sank into my brain that they were heading in our direction. The only ship on the entire horizon that was heading toward land was coming toward us. And not just toward us, but right at us.

I whacked Duffy on the shoulder to get his attention because he was half asleep. "What the hell?" he said. "Duffy," I replied, "Those lights are getting closer and they're coming right at us." That got his attention and the scowl disappeared from his face as he woke up and started watching the lights with me.

The ship was still miles off and we were trying not to get our hopes up too much because of all the near misses we had experienced during the day. The ship was still a long way off and it could change course at any time. Maybe it only looked like it was coming at us and was really not. I hoped against hope that we would finally be saved.

As the ship came within a couple miles, it dawned on me what I could now see. My heart started beating faster as I realized I could see a red and green light in the middle of the running lights at the base of my 'Christmas tree'. It was the bow light and, as any sailor knows, you can only see both red and green at the same time when the ship is heading directly toward you. This fricking ship was gonna run us over!

How ironic is that? We spend all day and night trying to get somebody's attention and no one can see us or gets anywhere near us. Now, we have a cargo ship bearing down on us who doesn't even know we're here and we have no way to signal him. We're gonna die being run over by a freighter. At least it would be quick. These thoughts went through my head in seconds and I had to laugh at myself for being so pessimistic, or maybe it was that dry sense of humor coming back.

I started to explain the bow light thing to Duffy and he looked at me like I had four eyes. 'I wish,' I thought to myself. My other two eyes are at the bottom of the ocean. "Duffy," I said, "When you can see the red and green of the bow light at the same time, it means it's coming directly at us. Its gonna run us over if we don't get out of the way!"

At this, he snapped completely awake and said, "Holy shit!" Dwayne, meanwhile, was pretty much oblivious to all of this and I hoped we could wake him up and weren't going to have to drag him out of the way. We would need all of our energy just to swim ourselves.

We watched the ship getting closer and larger and it was coming dead at us. I've never been shot at, but at least you can't see the bullet coming at you. This was torture... watching this five-hundred-foot beast heading directly at us and not knowing which way to go and whether or not we could move far enough and fast enough. At the same time, we wanted to get their attention, so we could be saved and not ground up into so much chum.

While all this was going on, we both worked on waking Dwayne up. He had been out of it for awhile and was slow to respond. With some prodding, shaking and a couple of slaps, he woke up. We brought him up to speed and his adrenalin kicked in, thank God. The ship was getting really close now and we had to make a decision as to which way to swim. Knowing my eyesight was piss poor, I told Duffy to pick a direction when he was ready and felt it was the right time to move. We unhooked our lifejackets from the life ring and just held on, waiting for Duffy to say 'go', while we all stared at this huge steel monstrosity bearing down on us.

Please, God, let us live through this.

As the ship bore down on us like a slow motion bullet out of a very large gun, I said my goodbyes to Anna and Joey, my parents and sister. I really didn't think we could get far enough away from this five-hundred-foot long and very wide ship to avoid being run over or sucked through the propellers.

Wrapped up in these thoughts, I didn't hear Duffy say, "Let's go ! This way!" Snapping out of my trance, I realized Duffy and Dwayne were already five yards away from me and heading to the starboard side of the ship. I let go of the lobster pot and swam for my life, which after all these hours of swimming, being dehydrated and hypothermic, felt as if I was moving in slow motion. Thank God for adrenalin, because I think that's all I had left.

Gasping for air as I caught up with Duffy and Dwayne, I glanced over my shoulder at the relentlessly on-coming ship and realized it wasn't going as fast as it could have been. Maybe we had a chance after all. At this point, the hull of the ship was not even ten feet away from me. We swam even harder as the bow began to pass us. We still needed to clear amidships, the widest part of the freighter. As the bow wave lifted us up a foot or two, I glanced back and saw the ship run right over our lobster pot marker and it disappeared in a frothy ball of foam under the hull. That could have been us, I thought. What if we had been unconscious?

By the time we realized we weren't going to be run over or sucked under the ship, about a third of its length had already passed us. We now focused on getting somebody's attention. We counted to three and repeatedly yelled "HELP!" in unison, for all we were worth. Portholes were gliding by, some open and some not. We continued to yell "HELP!" in unison, down the length of the freighter, hoping against hope that someone would hear us over the

rumbling of the big diesel engines. I could even feel their vibrations in the water. The running lights of the ship were shining on our faces. Dwayne and Duffy looked like shit and I'm sure I did, too. We were so close, only thirty feet or less from the side of the ship, we could actually read its name - the *Melvin H. Baker*.

Even with my poor eyesight, I could see the detail of its sides; the flaking bottom paint below the waterline, rivers of rust stains and hundreds of rivets, as she slid by. How could we be so close and yet no one could hear us screaming for our lives? So far, no one had so much as looked over the side of the ship or out of a porthole. There was no indication that anyone had heard or seen us.

The ship was about three-quarters past us and I could hear the loud sound of waves. I expected them to hit us as the ship went by. Knowing the backwash would soon cover us, we kept yelling as loud as we could. We were so close, we were actually in the rays of the ship's deck lights. Despair was starting to set in as we realized, even though we had almost been run over by this ship, we still couldn't be seen or heard. What I wouldn't have done for one more flare.

As the fantail of the ship slid toward us, we kept yelling, refusing to stop until we couldn't yell anymore..., and then a miracle occurred. There was a figure on the starboard side of the fantail, casually leaning on the railing, smoking a cigarette. As he passed by us and heard our screams, his head snapped around so fast he probably gave himself whiplash. He looked straight at us with a stunned expression on his face, then turned and bolted up some steps, disappearing into the ship. We had been seen and heard! We were going to be rescued! I'll never yell at anyone for smoking a cigarette again. Another link in that chain.

DAVE

I continued to find comfort in urinating every few minutes, which I couldn't figure out because we hadn't drunk nearly enough water to expel the amount that was coming out. I pulled my hand out of the water and, as I looked at the white wrinkled fingers, I could almost see the shape of the bones at each joint. I couldn't keep them out of the water for very long because they would get ice cold in the air in seconds. I reached down and touched my legs. I remember feeling the touch, but not knowing where the feeling was coming from because my hands felt numb.

The next thing I did was loosen my life jacket and slip my hand inside my shirt. I fumbled at the buttons for a minute, only to give up trying to get them unbuttoned. I reached under my shirt and felt my stomach. I began to feel queezy, just from feeling the lack of life in my hands and body. I pulled my hand out and raised it up in front of me and looked at it again. It was at that very minute I realized my body was dying and, in a few hours, I would be dead. My organs seemed as if they were part of the water and I could actually feel every beat of my heart inside me. I thought, the only real contact I ever had with death is when my uncle died and I remembered his hands... and how mine looked just like his.

Both Joe and I had to be contemplating the same thoughts because, for the longest time, neither one of us spoke to the other. I put my now freezing-cold hand back below the surface of the water. I turned away from Joe and, looking up into the full moon, began to cry for no other reason than it just felt good. There was nothing I could do to change our situation and I knew that crying never changed a thing, but it was just something that made me feel good – so I did it.

Around 10:30, I started shivering so bad that I started having convulsions and the only way I could stop them was to paddle my legs, as if I was riding a bicycle. These convulsions would come about three to five minutes after I would stop the paddling motion.

Sometimes I would let the convulsion go on because it was something different to feel. Joe didn't seem to be as cold as I was and I was beginning to wonder why he wasn't having convulsions. He still seemed to be ready to talk if I said anything.

I remember at one point that Joe kicked me by accident and he wasn't sure if he did or not. We both stopped moving for as long as we could, just to make sure it wasn't a shark bump. The way things were going, it would have been par for the course.

With the thought that I was going to die out here, I started thinking about everyone I was going to leave and, I must say, I wanted to cry again. I stopped myself because what I really wanted to do was think about it. Both my wife and I are born-again Christians and that's what made accepting the fact that I was going to die out here a lot easier. I began to believe that the Lord wanted it this way; otherwise, why would we have had three helicopter sightings, two of which should have been rescues?

I began to think about the last time I saw my daughters and I wondered if they were up right now. I worried about Barb and how she was handling everything that was going on. I remember reading in the *Bible* about the thief in the night, which is referring to death, and how if we knew when we were going to die, we would prepare for it. Therefore, no man knows when the thief will come. I almost had to laugh because I knew I would be dead in a few hours and, even though I had these few hours left, I still couldn't do anything to prepare for it. I had faith that the Lord would watch over my family and I also knew that He knew what was best. So, with that in my mind, I started thinking about the rest of my family and how they would handle my death.

All I had was my thoughts and my voice. This was the first time in my life that I experienced total helplessness and it reminded me of yet another *Bible* story in Luke, Chapter 16. It tells of a rich man who dies and goes to hell and, after finding himself in hell, he asked if he or someone he knew could go back and warn his brothers and sisters so that they would not end up where he was. I was experiencing that same helplessness and could only think about it.

I turned to Joe and asked him if he would mind if I prayed.

He turned his head toward me and said, "I've been praying to myself for hours – go right ahead."

We both closed our eyes and I just asked the Lord to send help and, if it be His will that we be rescued, please make it soon – and if not, please take care of our families. As we both said "Amen," Joe looked up and said, "We've done all we could. You know everything about me and I know everything about you. What can we do now?"

"You're asking me?" I said, sensing a little humor.

"Well, I've had a good life and, from what I hear, drowning isn't all that bad."

"Oh," I said. "I got a story for you. One time, when I was in high school, I went surfing after a hurricane and almost drowned. I really did," I said. "I fell off my board and was pulled under. I was rolled around so much that I didn't know which way was up or down."

"No kidding," said Joe. "One time I was caught in a wave when I was a kid."

Before Joe and I knew it, we were talking again and it was good because the subject was no longer about death and we had forgotten about the time. I would still feel the convulsions but, before they would take control of me, I would start paddling and wouldn't stop until the feeling was completely gone.

"What time is it getting to be?" I asked Joe, who pulled his hand out of the water to check.

"Not bad," he said. "It's five minutes to twelve."

Just then, I heard something and it alarmed me, because it was something I hadn't heard all night.

"Did you hear that?" I said to Joe.

"No, what?"

"Listen," I said, and we both went into our silent mode.

After about a minute, Joe said, "I don't hear anything."

"I know I heard something, just give it a minute," as we continued to listen.

"What does it sound like?" asked Joe.

"It was different. Sort of like..." That's as far as I got when, all of a sudden, we both jerked at the sound of a loud snort, followed by an explosive blast of air. I knew at once that it was a whale and it was probably as close to us as fifteen feet. The water all around us began to bubble with motion and currents that pulled and pushed us.

"Do you believe that?" I said. "I knew I heard something."

"I'm glad that's what you heard."

"Yeah, me too," I said. "That really gave me a scare."

I was thinking to myself again and, even though it was twelve o'clock at night (and I thought at ten that I'd never make twelve), I was really feeling weak. I started thinking there was no way I could make it until sun-up – and that was just when they would be resuming the search.

I had been watching the lights of tankers and ships off in the distance all night and found no interest at all in looking at the new ones that appeared. However, I just happened to turn and look at the area behind us to see a set of lights; I would say, about two miles away. The ship might as well have been a hundred miles away because it was out of yelling and swimming range, but it was definitely the closest out of all the ships that had passed us. As I watched, I noticed how well lit the topside deck was. It was at this minute I noticed that the ship seemed to be sitting still.

"Joe, does it look like that ship is moving?"

Having no interest in the ship at all, he half-turned and said, "What's the difference? It's too far away, anyway."

"Well, I'll tell you what . . . if he anchors for the night, I'm going to try and swim over to him."

"Why would he anchor out here?" Joe said.

"Beats me," I said. "Maybe he's got engine trouble. Maybe he wants to wait for sun-up before going up the Delaware."

"Who knows? Who cares? Just tell me, does he look like he's moving?"

"I'm sure he's not." Just as I said that, we could hear his motors shut off. This really got Joe's attention and we were now both facing the tanker.

"I'm going to make sure it anchors, because once I let go of this bamboo, I don't think I'll ever find it again – and it was hard enough to get to."

Joe said, "Let's give him a half-hour. If he's still there, then we'll try, but let's not take a chance on losing this flag. At least if we die here, they'll find us when they check the traps."

We both watched the ship as it stayed in the same spot for about five minutes. Then, without any warning, we heard the giant engines rumble on and, within a minute, the ship started moving. It was going to pass us, just like the last helicopter did and, as it did, neither Joe nor I found much comfort in watching the lights go by. We both saw it as just another disappointment. I was glad that the ship had stopped because, for a brief while there, we had a glimmer of hope. But that hope was now almost completely gone.

When the ship started to cross what was actually in front of us, I realized that I had lost my sense of direction; I no longer knew what direction land was in and it upset me. I don't know why, but it did. When I looked up at the stars, I began to feel dizzy. There was not a thing to do but start thinking about how long we would make it.

I asked Joe what time it was and he replied, "Twelve twenty-five."

I was losing the battle as far as keeping warm and hated the idea of moving, but if I didn't I would go into those uncontrollable convulsions that I was afraid wouldn't stop if I didn't paddle. I found that it was getting harder to stop them. I had to paddle almost all the time.

ART

Realizing that large ships don't stop on a dime, no matter how slow they are going, we watched in anticipation as she slid by us and kept going for what seemed like forever to us. It was now about 12:30 AM and we had been marinating in salt water for over seventeen hours We wanted out really badly. After going about a quarter mile beyond us, she appeared to be slowing down and, at the same time, began a slow ninety-degree turn to starboard. A few more minutes passed and, as she slowed even more, she made another ninety-degree turn ... again to starboard, bringing her a little closer to us.

When she came to a dead stop about a half mile away from us, all hell broke loose on deck. Every light on the ship seemed to snap on, with all available crew members on deck either helping to lower their lifeboat or looking out into the darkness trying to spot or hear us. We could hear the noises of our impending rescue; the clanking of winches and chains as they lowered the lifeboat, the Captain's instructions being broadcast over the PA system and the chattering of all the crew members in their native language.

When the lifeboat hit the water and they fired up its one-lung engine and started putt-putting in our general direction, we were finally beginning to believe that we were going to make it. We started swimming toward the ship and yelling at the top of our lungs. They weren't getting away from us now!

As we were making our way toward our rendezvous with the lifeboat, my thoughts turned to Dave and Joe. I prayed they were okay and had been picked up by the Coast Guard or another ship. My heart sank as I realized the odds of that happening were pretty steep. It was a straight-up miracle that we had been found by this wayward freighter. What are the odds of it happening twice in one night?

Just as I answered my own question with a 'slim to none,' I thought I heard voices off in the darkness... not coming from the ship. They were screaming the same words we were, "HELP, we're over here!" At first, I thought it was our voices echoing off the ship or some weird atmospheric anomaly. Then I heard the voices again, over all the splashing and yelling we were doing, and I realized they were coming from somebody besides us and the crew rescuing us. It had to be Dave and Joe. It just had to be. My heart lifted.

So I could hear them more clearly and get a fix on where they were, I told Duffy and Dwayne to shut up. They gave me the stink-eye and, before they could give me a load of crap, I explained that I had heard Dave and Joe yelling in the distance. They were surprised, but were more interested in getting into the lifeboat. No surprise there. We listened for a minute and I tried to get a bearing on their voices. I did this over and over as we kept swimming toward our rescuers. Each time I did, the results seemed to be the same. I couldn't tell how far away Dave and Joe were, but their voices were definitely coming out of the moon's sparkling reflection on that glassy smooth ocean. As the double-ended lifeboat with the one-lung engine putt-putted up to us, I filed that fact in my brain for later use. More links.

DAVE

The ship that had passed us was now about a mile away and neither Joe nor I paid any attention to it. Suddenly, there were sounds coming at us like nothing we had heard all night. We had to really strain to hear them. Within a minute, we could tell that it was screams. Both Joe and I were overcome with joy, not for any other reason than to know that our other shipmates were alive. There was no reason to think anything other than that. Being completely unaware of what was going on, we began to scream out their names. We started to forget all about our condition due to the excitement of knowing that they were alive.

The large tanker that had just passed us was now stopped again and we could actually see people on the deck, and more lights on than when we were thinking about swimming to it. The yells that we heard just minutes ago were too far away to be understood, but still close enough to be heard and they were almost constant now. I felt new life in my body and all of a sudden, out of nowhere, there was hope and joy – something that had been playing jokes on us all day. I was almost afraid to believe my eyes and ears as we strained to hear and see everything that was going on in front of us.

"Oh, my God, they're lowering a boat!"

"Where?" said Joe.

"Right on the side of the ship! See it?" I yelled.

"No. Where? You're right! You're right! Okay! My God, could this be it? Please, let this be it. Please, God!"

Both Joe and I kept repeating our comments as we watched the small boat being lowered into the ocean, still listening for our friends' yells for help. The small boat pulled away from the big ship and, as we watched, we would lose sight of it every now and then, due to the waves.

Within five minutes, Joe and I realized that we had better start our own little screaming session or they would never know we were here. With energy that I never knew I had, I let out the biggest and loudest "HELP!" I have ever let out in my life. Joe followed suit. We continued until we began to lose our strength, then we started alternating our yells for help. We yelled in the direction of the small boat, with our hands cupped around our cheeks, to try to amplify our voices.

160

When Joe was yelling and it was my turn to rest, I looked at my hands again. This time, they amused me more than scared me. For some reason, neither Joe nor I got tired of yelling, as we did it in turns. I really believed hearing each other yell gave each of us the strength needed to again yell when it was our turn. We had been hollering now for about twenty minutes and we were confident that they could hear our screams. As we watched and yelled, we noticed the small boat was returning to the ship. We weren't sure what was going on but, when the small boat started to be pulled up alongside the ship, we began to panic. We both started yelling again at the same time.

"They have to be hearing us!" I said to Joe in a hoarse voice.

"Then why aren't they coming for us?"

This was no time to reason and I joined right back in with Joe screaming for our lives - and we knew it.

The small boat was up on deck and I thought I would die when I heard the engines rumble. We never stopped yelling while the large ship made some strange turns right in front of us, then just stood there. We continued to yell until almost all of our strength was gone. Joe would yell an occasional "HELP" and, as soon as I felt good enough, I would let out my best shout. It was really scary thinking that at any minute the ship was going to disappear in front of us, but it didn't. Every now and then, the motors would race.

"Why aren't they coming for us?" we asked each other, as if we knew the answer.

"They haven't left. They must have radioed the Coast Guard or something."

"Well, just keep doing what we're doing with the yelling then," I said.

ART

None of the rescuers in the lifeboat spoke English so, with hand signals and gestures, they indicated they were going to pull us into the boat one at a time. After the crew grabbed each of us by our arms and hoisted us up and over the gunnels like three large tuna fish, we collapsed onto the benches of the boat, unable to move. Our arms and legs felt like they were lead. After floating in water for eighteen hours and becoming so weak, gravity now demanded more energy than we had available.

I tried to explain to the crew that there were two more men in the water and what direction they were in, but the language barrier was not helping. Finally, they seemed to understand and, with gestures of their own, indicated that they wanted to unload the three of us onto the freighter before searching for Dave and Joe. I looked around and realized the lifeboat was full and two more men probably wouldn't fit. So they turned the boat toward the mother ship and off we putted. This thing wasn't going to set any speed records. I could still faintly hear Dave and Joe's voices over the noise of the engine and hoped they realized we weren't going to leave them.

After about ten minutes, we approached the side of the *Melvin H. Baker* and our rescuers indicated they wanted us to climb up the cargo net ladder hanging over the side so they could go and search for Dave and Joe. Our collective asses got about four inches off the bench and we all collapsed. We couldn't even stand up. To make matters worse, the convulsions were kicking in again after sitting in the boat and being exposed to the cool night air. We were shaking pretty badly. The crew realized there was no way in hell we were climbing up that net and made preparations to hoist the entire lifeboat up onto the main deck.

After we reached the main deck, we were each assisted by two crew members who carried us down the side of the ship and up into their galley where we collapsed into chairs, unable to move except for the shaking. Although we couldn't speak with anyone, these guys knew what to do. They brought us towels, blankets and dry clothes from their lockers and helped us dry off and change. Then, an endless stream of hot coffee, soup, donuts and cakes were brought for our consumption.

You can't imagine how good it felt to touch something warm and eat something after being that cold and hungry for that long. While we were gorging ourselves on coffee and sugary foods, I thought of Dave and Joe still out there. I hoped the crew had re-launched the lifeboat and were looking for them but, because no one spoke English, we had no idea what was happening. I was aware the ship was still dead in the water, so I knew we weren't leaving them... no way.

* *

COAST GUARD REPORT

AT 1:50 A.M., COAST GUARD THIRD DISTRICT COMMUNICATIONS CENTER RECEIVED A RADIO TRANSMISSION FROM THE CAPTAIN OF THE VESSEL MELVIN H. BAKER REPORTING THAT THEY HAD RESCUED THREE OF FIVE PEOPLE IN THE WATER AND ASKING FOR ASSISTANCE IN FINDING THE TWO REMAINING SURVIVORS. U.S. COAST GUARD BASE CAPE MAY LAUNCHED A HELICOPTER AT 1:55 A.M. AND WAS ENROUTE TO THE BAKER.

AT 1:55 A.M., A PHONE CALL WAS MADE IN RESPONSE TO AN EARLIER CALL OF AN OVERDUE BOAT FROM A MRS. BARBARA JONES.

* *

DAVE

After all of the close calls we had with being rescued today, we just couldn't take anything for granted. It had been a half-hour since the small boat had been pulled up and the large tanker was still just about a mile away. Whenever a negative thought came into my mind, I would yell. I couldn't feel the cold any longer and it seemed a lot easier to gather up strength to yell. I kept searching the sky for lights, but it was very hard to tell because of the stars; they all looked as if they were moving, if you looked hard enough.

It had now been forty-five minutes and the ship made no effort to come closer or to lower its lifeboat again. We continued an occasional chant for help. Still not knowing which way land was made it very difficult watching the sky for helicopter lights. I felt we were going to be saved now and all I could do was hope that it would be soon. I stopped yelling for a few minutes because I felt myself getting light-headed. So, I just tried to search the sky for lights.

It seemed to have come out of nowhere, but before Joe and I realized it, a set of lights appeared about a mile behind the ship. Within seconds, a helicopter was hovering over the ship, just a few feet above the bridge, which was completely lit up from the four large floodlights that were under the helicopter. Both Joe and I were happy; maybe the happiest we'd ever been in our lives.

As we watched, the next few minutes started with the helicopter traveling in a circle around the ship, making the circle larger as it came around the ship. We could see the large patch of light that the floodlights made on the surface of the water and the noise of the helicopter was getting louder every time it came closer to us. We waited in total anticipation of being spotted.

The helicopter finally got to the point in its circle where we thought they would have to see us and we watched as the large patch of light moved closer toward us, missing us by only fifty feet. We waited for the next pass, thinking this has got to be it. This time it missed us by an easy hundred feet, but it was on the other side of us! That meant it would be even farther away on the next pass. Fear started to creep back into us as we watched the helicopter stop the search and head back to the ship.

"What are we going to do now?" Joe yelled.

"Just sit tight," I said. I couldn't believe I had just comforted Joe.

* *

COAST GUARD REPORT

AT 1:15 A.M., COAST GUARD HELICOPTER REPORTED THAT THEY HAD REACHED THE MELVIN H. BAKER AND WERE BEGINNING TO SEARCH THE AREA FOR THE TWO MISSING MEN. AFTER A TWENTY MINUTE SEARCH OF THE AREA, THE HELICOPTER WAS CALLED BACK TO THE BAKER TO TALK TO ONE OF THE SURVIVORS AND GIVEN DIRECTIONS ON WHAT AREA TO SEARCH.

* *

ART

After awhile, the Captain and his wife appeared in the galley. He introduced himself and his wife, in English. It was music to my ears. We could finally communicate with someone. He explained that they had not re-launched the lifeboat, but had called the Coast Guard and were awaiting their helicopter's arrival on scene; that they would search for Dave and Joe. The Captain said he was afraid he would run you guys over so he planned on just staying in the same location until the Coast Guard arrived.

At this point, I didn't know whether Dave and Joe were

drifting or had also found a marker to hang onto. I was worried that they might drift off and not be where I thought they were. I prayed they had stayed put. The Captain excused himself and said he was returning to the bridge to await the helicopter's arrival. Before he left, I tried to make him understand that I had an idea of where to look for Dave and Joe. I'm not sure he got it, but he said he would send someone down for me when the helicopter arrived.

Taking some comfort that the Coast Guard was on the way and there was nothing else I could do until they arrived, I attacked the coffee and donuts again. We were still shaking and ravenous for fuel. It seemed like we would never warm up again. The three of us looked at each other and agreed we all looked like half-drowned rats, but we rejoiced in being alive and fortunate to have been rescued by these very generous people. Now we just needed to find Dave and Joe.

Another half hour had passed when I heard the faint sounds of a chopper in the distance. It gradually became louder until it was right over the ship. After several minutes, it began to move and appeared to be going in circles around the ship, each circle a little farther away. I realized they were looking for Dave and Joe. Somebody get me to the radio room!

Finally, a crew member approached me and motioned for me to follow him. I went to jump up and realized there was no 'jump' in me. Even after being on the ship and "warming up" for an hour or so, there was no way I could stand on my own, let alone walk and climb stairs. He looked at me with understanding in his eyes and motioned for one of his buddies to come over and help carry me up to the radio room. He smiled at me and just kept repeating, "Okay, okay, okay."

When we reached the bridge, the Captain greeted me and shook my hand, then directed me to the radio room, which was a few feet away and off to the side of the bridge. I was handed a headset and told the chopper pilot was on the line. I introduced myself as one of the survivors and proceeded to tell him to bring the

chopper over the ship, turn it toward the reflection of the moon and follow it like the yellow brick road. Dave and Joe are out in that reflection somewhere.

I stayed on the radio, listening as the pilot brought the chopper over the ship, turned it, flipped on their searchlights and slowly headed off into the night. As I stood there watching the helicopter continue the search, I could hear the captain issue orders (in Chinese). Looking down, I could tell that the ship was remaining stationary, pretty much like being tied up to a lobster pot flag, which is not as easy as you might think it would be for a five hundred foot tanker.

Within minutes, the pilot radioed back that they had been spotted and rescue procedures were under way. They were plucking Dave and Joe out of the water and would be taking them directly to Burdette Tomlin Memorial Hospital in Cape May. They would then return to pick the rest of us up in an hour or so.

Elation doesn't describe the emotion that overwhelmed me at that moment when it hit me that we had all survived. I wept like a baby, realizing that we were all going to see our families again..., that we weren't going to die tonight after all . The Captain came over to me and patted me on the back, knowingly.

The events of the entire day washed over me, and I said a short prayer to God thanking Him for getting all of us through this ordeal. Only He could put a chain together that long and make all the things that had to happen for us to be rescued today happen. It was truly a miracle and no one will ever convince me otherwise.

DAVE

All three of the other guys – Art, Dwayne and Duffy – had been picked up in the lifeboat and were now on the ship, where the crew had carried them down to the galley, wrapped them in blankets and started filling them with warm coffee and food.

As Joe and I watched the helicopter hovering over the boat, we wondered what was going to happen next, when suddenly the helicopter turned and started heading right toward us. In less than a minute, we were in the circle of the bright searchlights. Not knowing what to do next, we just tried to accustom ourselves to the light and noise of the helicopter, not to mention the salty spray that was being stirred up.

The noise was so loud now that we could feel it, and we knew something was about to happen. The pilot landed the helicopter right on the water, maybe twenty feet from us, and I could see the man in the side door giving us the 'come over' sign. There were lights on the side of the helicopter and floodlights beneath it. Combined with the thunderous beating of the rotor blades, churning up the water into a frantic mist, the light and sound was an unbelievable assault on the senses.

As Joe and I fumbled at the belts that had kept us secured to the bamboo pole all day, I couldn't help thinking, 'Is this all really happening?' It was an unbelievable sight. As we let go of the bamboo pole and tried swimming toward the open door of the helicopter, the current that had pushed us all day ripped us off in a direction away from the helicopter.

The captain was watching from the side window and, when we started to disappear into the darkness, he brought the helicopter around to where we were drifting and positioned the open side door right where we would drift into it.

Once, I saw a movie in which the actor was telling a story of how he had been in the water for three days while sharks attacked the shipmates all around him. He said the scariest moment was on that third day, when he was just about to be rescued, thinking any moment the shark would take him next. Well, that's all I could think about as I tried to push Joe's back when we got to the door of the helicopter. I was overcome with the fear that, as I was pushing Joe into the door of the chopper, a shark would come up through the well-lit water and snatch me down into the depths... and I would never make it home.

Joe was pulled up into the darkness of the chopper and I kicked, thinking that this is going to be like climbing out of a pool without a ladder. I was instead pulled out of the water and into a solid black compartment. As my eyes focused, it began to look like what I always thought a UFO would look like inside. Before I could say or do anything, a Martian-looking person came over and firmly, but gently, pushed me down and began to strap me to a seat next to Joe, who was already wrapped in a blanket. I really felt like we were in the Twilight Zone and everything that was going on was just a dream.

* *

COAST GUARD REPORT

AT 1:45 A.M., COAST GUARD HELICOPTER RADIOED COMMAND CENTER AT CAPE MAY BASE THAT THEY LOCATED AND PICKED UP TWO MEN OUT OF THE OCEAN. AFTER TAKING THEIR VITAL SIGNS, IT WAS DETERMINED THEY WOULD RETURN IMMEDIATELY TO BASE TO DROP OFF THESE TWO MEN. A REQUEST WAS MADE FOR MEDICAL TRANSPORTATION TO BE READY. THE HELICOPTER WOULD THEN RETURN TO THE BAKER FOR THE OTHER THREE SURVIVORS. ANOTHER CALL WAS MADE TO MRS. BARBARA JONES, INFORMING HER THAT ALL FIVE MEN HAD BEEN RESCUED.

* *

The noise was awesome and, as the door slammed shut, the man in what looked like a sky-diver suit with a life jacket and helmet on gave the pilot the thumbs-up sign. The noise that I thought couldn't get any louder doubled. Next, a blanket was wrapped around me and a very serious young man started medical procedures on me: first, thermometer in the mouth; next, pulse. I looked over at Joe, who was having the same thing done to him by a another paramedic.

After our vital signs were checked and written down, I grabbed the young man's hand and looked him in the eye and said, "Thank you." He smiled and said something that I just couldn't hear because of the noise. Next, he reached over with a set of headphones and put them on my head and started talking. As I looked at him, I could see his mouth moving, but couldn't hear anything. I turned my head toward the front and the pilot was looking back and talking. I still couldn't hear anything. I reached up and pulled one side of the headphones off and I could feel the water coming out of my ear. When I put it back on, I could hear the crews' voices now and, while talking to them, emptied the other ear out.

"Thank you," is all I could mutter at first, and they all smiled.

Then the pilot said, "You guys are lucky to be alive."

It was good to see that all the guys on the helicopter were enjoying what they were doing. It's as if they were just as happy as we were. I still couldn't feel anything and, as the helicopter lifted up into the sky, I could see the ship that had radioed the helicopter. As we reached a height that was above the deck of the ship, I asked if the other guys from our boat were all okay, but got no response. I asked again, because I could still hear the helicopter crew. I was just about to grab the man's arm, as he was still writing on the clipboard, when I heard a voice on the headset say, "If you want to talk, you have to press the small button under the mouthpiece."

I felt a little foolish, but it didn't stop me from asking over the crew talk if our friends were alright. The pilot, who was in the position to talk to me and half look at me, turned, smiled and said, "Everyone is alright and, if you look down on the deck behind the bridge, you'll see one of them. It seems that they couldn't find anyone on board who spoke English well enough to give us directions, so your friend insisted on coming up to the bridge to tell us where he last heard your yells. It appears he refused to leave the bridge until he knew you were both picked up and safe."

As he turned the helicopter, I could see the figure of a man with a blanket wrapped around him and two men helping him down a set of steps. I don't think I will ever be able to express in words or action how happy I was to know that we all were well and accounted for. I heard some loud clicks on the headset and saw the pilot of the helicopter talking on the radio, but couldn't hear him on the headset, so I pressed the small button and asked what was happening.

The medic looked up and said, "We're going to take you guys back to base and then come back for your buddies. The pilot is just letting the captain of the freighter know."

"Won't we all fit in here?" I asked.

"We have got to get you guys some medical attention. It will take another forty-five minutes to pick them up and in thirty we'll have you in the hospital and be on our way back."

"But I feel fine," I said to the corpsman.

"You shouldn't," he said. "Your body temperature is only ninety-one and you are in big-time need of fluids. So just sit back and relax. We know our job."

I looked over at Joe, who was leaning against a wire mesh divider, and asked how he was feeling.

With as serious a look as I've ever seen on Joe, he said, "Just thankful to be alive," and he reached over and patted my hand.

As soon as I heard the clicking on the radio that I had heard earlier, I looked back at the pilot, who was being very professional and giving out orders that were being followed 'to the T' by the crew. I could now feel the helicopter being taken over by the power of the engines and it reminded me of the way Duffy's boat responded to the power it had. As we lifted higher into the sky, we watched the ship get smaller. Then the helicopter turned and we had to turn our heads to look out the side window. We pulled away from the ship at a considerable rate of speed. We watched until all that could be seen was a patch of lights on the dark horizon, much the same sight as the tankers and ships that had passed us all night. I couldn't stop thinking of all that had happened in the last hour-and-a-half and what was happening now.

ART

As the two crew members carried me back down to the galley, I heard the chopper make one last pass over the ship before taking Dave and Joe into Cape May. My friends were safe and on their way home. We were ALL safe and on our way home. The realization was so overpowering and so contradictory to our dire situation just a short time ago that tears of joy streamed down my face yet again. I got the feeling there were going to be a lot of tears of joy and thankfulness shed for awhile. I composed myself and could sense that my entire outlook on life was going to undergo a major overhaul in the coming weeks. For now, first things first... more donuts and coffee!

My escorts got me back to the galley and I filled Duffy and Dwayne in about Dave and Joe's rescue and transport to the hospital. They were happy to hear the good news, but their response was less than overwhelming. I sensed that they may be feeling a little guilty about their behavior earlier in the day. I let it slide and then explained that we would be on board for approximately another hour until the chopper returned to pick us up. As I finished bringing them up to speed, we heard the ship's big diesel engines begin to pick up r.p.m's and could feel the ship shudder and begin to move again.

Over the next hour or so, while we tried to warm up and get some strength back, we discussed most of the events of the last twenty-four hours (somehow the two disappearing sodas didn't come up) and how extremely lucky we were to be sitting on this freighter, right now, sipping hot coffee and eating donuts. Just two hours ago, we were literally dying slowly in the ocean's grasp; cold, alone, dehydrated, and without any hope of rescue. I don't think we would have made it until daylight, let alone until that lobster boat captain made his rounds to check his traps. I couldn't wait to see Dave and Joe.

Just as we could hear the copter approaching the ship to pick us up, the Captain arrived to say goodbye and wish us well. We thanked him and the crew for all they had done for us. He was very gracious and reiterated how very lucky we were. Then he explained that the Coast Guard was going to pick us up in a rescue basket, one at a time, while the ship continued on its way to port. Sounds exciting doesn't it? After the day we had, this should be a piece of cake.

DAVE

Suddenly, I was hit with a wave of concern about Barbara and, with a jumping up type motion, looked for the closest member of the crew. This really scared the corpsman, because he unbelted himself and came to me as if something was wrong.

"Has anyone notified my wife that we are okay?" I asked.

"Are you alright?" came over the radio, as the corpsman put his hand on my shoulder. It was hard to focus on his face, as I tried to look into his eyes. He had a helmet on with lightning bolts coming away from the opening, a large sun shield pulled up in a chin strap that was hanging, and a radio receiver at his mouth.

"I'm fine," I said, pressing the button. "Has anyone notified our wives?"

With that, he returned to the corner he had just flown out of and strapped himself back in. Then he answered that headquarters knew the rescue was under way and he was sure they were keeping everyone informed.

"Please try not to move around too much. We'll be landing soon."

We had been flying about fifteen minutes and the shoreline lights were just starting to come into sight. As land started to become unmistakably visible, the pilot started to issue orders. With eagerness, the crew began to make arrangements for landing. We were still over the ocean, but could easily make out the shapes of things that were coming up, as we neared the well-lit shoreline.

I still couldn't move my fingers too well and was glad that it didn't take too much to press the radio button. As we came closer to land, the pilot got especially busy giving out orders, and it sure was good to know that we didn't have to do any of them. It was too hard to get into a position that would have allowed a view of the ground underneath us.

We had no sooner gotten over land when one of the crew opened the side door – the same side door that had been used to pull us in from the water. Now we could see the ground and, boy, was it getting close fast! Suddenly, there was a great abundance of light and I could see the area that we were landing in was being flooded with red flashing lights, the kind on a cop car or ambulance.

Even with the headphones on, the noise was deafening once the door was opened. I wondered if the helmets were better because I had to depend on sign language if I asked anything of Joe, who was still balled up and strapped in. I was glad to see two ambulances as we turned to come in for a landing.

What a sight the landing pad was at night. The windsock was lit up and there was a large ring of lights that surrounded a Coast Guard vehicle, with the ambulance on the outside of the circle. It really was impressive to see the crew performing the way they did to complete this rescue mission. Next to the ambulance was a group of people standing ready with the portable stretchers. The closer we got to the ground, the louder the noise got and I didn't remember the helicopter being that loud.

As I felt the wheels bounce down on the landing pad, I could see all kinds of activity, both inside and outside the helicopter. Two men came over and unstrapped Joe and took him to the door. I was surprised when I saw one of the men jump out and almost disappear; all that could be seen was the top of his helmet. I turned my head down and started taking the straps off of me, thinking that all I had to do was jump out like the first guy did. It wasn't that high, I thought, comparing it to some of the decks I had jumped off of in the past.

I wasn't aware of the fact that I had hardly any movement at all in my body. As I pulled myself up to a standing position, not wanting to give up the blanket that was wrapped around me, I moved toward the door and looked down, still thinking that I was fine. I looked for Joe, who had just exited in front of me. When I put my head out the door of the helicopter, I found out what real noise was. Although the blades were far above my head, I still bent my head down as a natural reaction. Still looking for Joe, I saw him being strapped to one of the ambulance beds. I positioned myself to jump out. As I started to lift my leg, I felt the other leg give out and, in an instant, I was nothing more than a pile of wet clothes and weak flesh wrapped in a blanket under the door.

Everyone came running over and picked me up in a way that they must have thought I was seriously hurt. I really could have been, but knew after I fell that I wasn't. I couldn't understand why I couldn't move, though. I remembered being in the water and having no problem moving at all. Now it was hard to even bend my arm.

As I was being strapped in the bed, I watched the helicopter door slam shut and the engines started to power up. I got my hand out from under the strap, enough that I was able to give a wave goodbye to the crew. The guy at the side door waved back and I saw the pilot smile and give me the thumbs-up sign. In less than thirty seconds, they were up and back on course to the tanker to pick up the remaining guys.

As they lifted me up and started putting me in the back of the ambulance, I thanked the people, who were all volunteers, for what they had done for me and for what they were doing. They all laughed and said, "Thank us after we get you to the hospital."

I looked over at Joe and said, "How are you doing, buddy?"

He turned his head and said, "Thank you for staying back with me."

I laughed and replied, "You'd better think about that. I'm the one who invited you on this trip."

The rest of the way to the hospital, we talked about whether our wives would be there or not, and how soon we thought it would be before we saw our shipmates. I asked the attendant if they were dropping us off and going back for the others. She said that they probably wouldn't because the ambulance that stayed was big enough to fit the three guys they were expecting. Then she said that this ambulance was actually big enough to have taken all five of us at the same time, but from our medical report, we needed to get to the hospital sooner.

"Did you know your body temperature was ninety-one? By the way, why are you two yelling?"

Both Joe's and my ears were still ringing from the helicopter ride and neither of us realized we were talking so loud.

ART

We were escorted to the main deck and waited for the Coast Guard helicopter to line up and get in synch with the ship's direction and speed. I took in the view of the ship's deck stretched out before me. This thing was huge, and the rumble of the engines was loud, and it was everywhere you went. No wonder it took a guy on the fantail smoking a cigarette less than fifty feet away from us to see and hear us. Had it not been for him, we'd still be floating around out there. I started to shake again, only this time I didn't think it was from being cold.

* *

COAST GUARD REPORT

AT 2:20 A.M., COAST GUARD HELICOPTER REPORTED THAT IT HAD RETURNED TO THE VESSEL, MELVIN H. BAKER, AND WAS IN THE PROCESS OF SETTING UP TO HOIST THE REMAINING SURVIVORS INTO THE HELICOPTER. AFTER A MEDICAL CHECK, THE DECISION WAS MADE TO LAND AT BURDETTE TOMLIN MEMORIAL HOSPITAL, WHERE THE OTHER TWO MEN WERE BEING TREATED. THE HELICOPTER WOULD THEN RETURN TO BASE.

* *

The Coast Guard hoisted a corpsman down to the deck to assist us into the rescue basket, and to make sure we were in and secure. These guys were good and made it all look so easy. Duffy and Dwayne were hoisted up, one at a time, as I watched in wonder at how smoothly it went. The chopper was right overhead and was in perfect unison with the ship. Between the rumble of the ship's big diesels and the roar of the chopper's rotor blades, communication was limited to hand signals.

Finally, it was my turn. I turned and waved to the Captain and crew, mouthing the words 'Thank you' as the corpsman helped me into the basket and strapped me in. He stepped back and gave the thumbs up sign to the hoist operator and off I went. On my way up, I just tried to absorb as much of my surroundings as possible. I gazed down at the five-hundred-foot, plus, *Melvin H. Baker*, fully illuminated and cruising toward the Delaware Bay, and then to the surrounding glassy, black ocean with the full moon still sparkling off its surface all the way out to the horizon. A dozen or more freighters were cruising up and down the coast, oblivious of the life and death drama we had just experienced. Even after all we'd been through, I still thought it was the most beautiful night I'd ever seen on the water.

I looked in all directions and was overwhelmed at the vastness of the ocean. Other than the *Melvin H. Baker*, the helicopter and the distant ships on the horizon, there was not another light to be seen anywhere, in any direction... nothing. We had to be on that particular lobster pot marker, AND the *Melvin H. Baker* had to run over that particular marker, AND have a crewman with a tobacco craving at THAT particular time of night, AND he had to be on the starboard side of the fantail to hear and see us. Odds makers wouldn't even consider giving odds on our survival under these conditions. And these are just a few of the links in the chain of events that had to happen in a certain order and a certain way for us to be in that particular place at that particular time to be rescued. It was mind-boggling, as much as it was humbling.

As another corpsman pulled the basket inside the helicopter, I saw Dwayne and Duffy huddled up under blankets, being checked by a medic. I was helped out of the basket and then they sent it back down for the corpsman on deck. They handed me another blanket and a headset so we could hear each other over the roar of the engines.

He asked me how I felt. "Really tired, really cold, and really happy to be going home," I replied. He laughed, shaking his head, and asked if there was anyone they could call to notify that I was okay. I gave him Anna's name and our home phone number. I kept thinking over and over, "I'm going home. I'm going home." Never had those words meant so much to me.

After a flight of about thirty minutes, we landed on the tarmac at Burdette Tomlin Memorial Hospital in Cape May. We still needed help walking and were assisted into the hospital where we were taken down to the emergency area and treated for hypothermia and exposure. Even after two hours aboard the *Baker*, with dry clothes and warm food, our core body temperatures were at 92.5, and we were still shaking. I didn't think it would ever stop.

CHAPTER NINE

DAVE

When we got to the hospital, there was a group of nurses and a few more doctors than I expected. When they wheeled us into the emergency room, I asked what was going on and one of the nurses said that everyone wanted to see the guys that were rescued from being in the water all day. As we arrived, two very nice nurses were working busily on both of us, asking us general questions about our health and how we felt right now.

I stopped her routine and said to her, "Could you please do me a favor?"

"What is it?" she asked sincerely.

"Could you call my wife and tell her we're alright and not to worry."

"What's your number?" she asked.

I gave it to her, then Joe, who was no more than a few feet away, asked her if she would have Barb call his wife. She turned to Joe and asked, "Would you like me to call her, too?"

Joe said, "No, that's alright."

One nurse disappeared while the other was taking our clothes off and drying us. As soon as the nurse returned, she gave us the news that she talked to my wife, totally assuring her that we were fine. She also said Barb would take care of calling Joe's wife. Then we were both hooked up to heart monitors and covered up with blankets. What a great sensation it was to feel the warm room and the dry blankets. I could sense the feeling coming back into my body and tried moving my arm, which moved at the elbow, but when I tried to lift the whole arm, it wouldn't work.

Joe and I were quiet and the only disturbance was, every few minutes, we would hear a voice say, "Where are they?" and two seconds later a head would pop in through the white curtains to see what we looked like. It felt so good just to lie there and relax that when one of the nurses popped her head through the curtain and asked if we'd like a cup of coffee or something from the cafeteria, both Joe and I waited, hoping the other would answer. The nurse started to pull her head back out of the curtains, assuming we didn't want anything.

"What can we have?" I asked. I've got money in my wallet and neither one of us has eaten all day."

This shocked the nurse, who came back in and asked if we liked chicken soup.

"Please!" we both responded.

It turned out that the nurse gave us her dinner, which she brought from home for herself. Everyone was being extremely nice to us. After being fed by the nurse, I tried lifting my arm and, aside from a little pain, was able to move it up. I asked Joe if he had any trouble moving and he said he had a little.

"Maybe it's that fall you took," he said.

"What fall?" asked the nurse and I began to tell her about the fall out of the helicopter.

"If you can't move it, we'll take an x-ray," she said.

"I think it will be okay. It's just that earlier I couldn't move it at all and now I'm starting to get my feeling back."

"Well, that's because your body temperature was so low, but it's climbing quite quickly now."

I asked her if she heard anything about the other three guys or if she knew where they were now.

"No, but they'll have to come through here first, so you'll be the first to know when they get here."

With that, she said, "Now you guys relax and just take it easy." She opened the curtain, maybe about a foot, and went out of the room. This gave us a perfect view of the entire emergency area. As I lay there on the bed with nothing on but a hospital pajama top and a pile of blankets, I began to check out different parts of my body. I was surprised when I saw my face in the mirror because I hadn't expected it to be swollen. I looked at my arms and shoulders and they were still wrinkled. I looked over at Joe and felt better when I saw puffiness around his eyes and cheeks. The reality of being rescued had not really set in yet. It was still hard to believe all that had happened in just the last hour-and-a-half.

Reaching down and feeling the wires that were connected to my chest, I thought about how just hours earlier I could feel my heart beating in the water. It was so good to be warm and dry. After examining my chest, without looking at it, I lowered my hand down to my stomach and got a little queasy when I pressed on it. The next place I put my hand shocked me because of what I was expecting to find, but didn't; I touched my groin area and felt nothing. I panicked for a second and lost control of myself. Sitting up in bed, I flipped the covers off and looked down. As I did this, I ripped some of the wires off my chest and the heart monitor alarm went off with a loud buzz. This sent both nurses back into our room. As they arrived, I pulled the covers back and tried to answer her questions, trying to get time to ask her a few of my own. When she was assured that I was alright, she asked what happened, but before I could answer her, a doctor was on the scene.

While the nurse was reattaching the wires to my chest, I looked over at Joe. He was laughing uncontrollably in his bed. As serious as I could be, I asked Joe if he had... That's as far as I got when Joe answered, "Mine's not there either," and went back to laughing again at my reaction.

The doctor who was standing there asked what happened and I told him I was a little upset over the fact my penis wasn't anywhere to be found, and it had upset me to the point where I sat up and pulled the wires out. He assured me everything was okay and it was quite normal and not to worry. By now, Joe was cracking jokes and both of us were laughing. It felt so good to have a normal reaction or, better yet, function normally; almost every reaction or emotion we had up to this point had been an effort.

After about five minutes of laughing, Joe looked over to me and asked if I ever thought laughing could feel so good. It was real! We really were safe; the nightmare was over and it felt so good to be alive.

We were both slipping back into a quiet period when we heard a lot of commotion. Before I could lift my head to see what was going on, the nurse who had given us her dinner popped her head in to our area and announced that our buddies were here. Both Joe and I were up on our elbows watching. We watched the nurses wheel in more heart monitors and were really surprised when we saw three guys walk in.

"You guys alright?" yelled Joe, which caught all three by surprise as they stopped and looked in our direction. They all smiled and started toward us, but were headed off by the nurses, who took their blankets and began directing them to different beds. As the blankets came off, both Joe and I let out a little laugh, which was caused by the sight of the clothes they had on. The last time I saw Duffy, he was wearing a nice set of clothes and very fancy storm gear – the same for Art and Dwayne. Now, they were dressed in clothes that the ship's crew had given them and they looked pretty funny.

Joe and I also noticed that they looked in a lot better physical condition than we did.

As we watched the nurses checking temperatures and hooking up the monitors, we asked them questions like, "Would you guys like a cup of coffee? You can get it here."

Art rolled over on his side and said, "We've been drinking coffee and eating on that ship for the past two-and-a-half hours. All I want to do is get home."

Joe looked over to me and said, "Boy, they really look good!"

I said, "You've got to remember, we were in the water another hour and a half more than they were, and I'm feeling better with every minute that passes."

As I said that, I heard a voice that sounded very familiar and, turning, I saw my wife, Barbara. She was standing with her back to me, looking at Joe, then Dwayne and then Art. With a touch of nervousness, she asked where I was.

"Hi, baby," I said, which made her turn around only to turn white and ask, "What's wrong? Why are you back there?"

"Come here, just come here," I said, holding back my tears at the sight of hers. All she could do was just stand there and cry. The next voice I heard was that of my father-in-law, who had driven her to the hospital. He came up from behind her and sort of guided her to the bed, where she just hung on me.

Through her tears, she asked, "How come you're in the bed, all bundled up, when the other guys all have clothes on?"

"We've been here about an hour," Joe answered Barbara in a very comforting voice.

Her next questions was, "Is everyone alright?"

"We're all fine," I said.

Barbara got up and went over to Joe's bed and said, "I spoke to your wife and daughter and they are on their way." She then told Dwayne that she had contacted his wife, and she was also on the way.

"Duffy, I hope I did right, because I didn't know who to call so I called your wife," and Duffy just rolled his eyes and said, "What a day!" then turned back to Barb and said, "Thank you very much."

Next, she walked over to Art's bed, leaned over, hugged him and said, "I called Anna and she's fine, but asked if we could bring you home."

Art smiled and said, "It's either you bring me home or I'm walking," which gave us all a good laugh and helped to stop some of the tears.

The nurse came back to my bedside and took my temperature again, just as Joe's wife and one of his daughters showed up.

I asked the nurse if we would be able to go home and, with doubtful eyes she said, "You might be admitted, but I'll check with the doctor."

The doctor was somewhere in the emergency room and in a few minutes was next to the bed. He checked my pulse and asked how I felt.

"Just a little sore," I said.

With that he said, "I'll leave it up to you. If you want to go home, you can. If you feel weak, we'll put you in a room."

My wife was very upset and asked why the doctor was so concerned with us. He turned and said, "We've monitored their hearts and brought their temperatures up. They have been very stable since they got here. The only thing we could do is give them a bed to rest in."

By now, Dwayne's wife was there, as well as Duffy's wife, along with friends, and everyone was in the emergency room. The doctor who had just spoken to Barb walked into the center of the room and loudly announced that he wanted everyone to go outside and wait for us. This didn't go over too well and, when no one left, he changed his orders to 'one person at a time to each patient'. Upon seeing the compromise, some of the people started to obey.

Barb asked if we wanted to stay, saying that she could come back for us in the morning.

"No! I want home! How about you, Joe?"

Things were starting to happen quickly again and, as the nurse disconnected Dwayne, Duffy and Art from the monitors, they wheeled them out of the emergency room. After removing all three of them from the room, she headed over to our beds. I was feeling much better and, as I had the wires removed from me, I asked if there were pajama bottoms that I could borrow. The nurses joked around with me and pretended there were none and, just before wheeling us out, gave me and Joe pajama bottoms. Once in the hallway, we could talk with everyone and it was very obvious that we were all so glad to see each other.

There were plenty of tears, and Barbara's father was running around taking everybody's picture. At some point, although I'm sure Fred didn't realize it, he had to be stopped; he was now asking if he could get us all together for a group picture.

Then a nurse came out and asked if we would all get the paperwork signed that would allow us to leave the hospital. All the wives went forward and, one-by-one, returned. We all looked at each other and promised to meet the next day to discuss everything that had happened.

One-by-one, a car pulled up to the emergency room entrance and a group of people got in – with one member of the group wrapped in blankets. Sitting in the back seat of Barbara's dad's car, with Barb next to me, I could see Fred's face in the mirror. It was full of excitement and, as he asked me questions, I could see him just imagining he was there. I was glad I was in the back seat with Barb. Poor Art, in the front seat with Fred, got bombarded with question after question.

Fred was trying to relive our experience. He had no idea what a nightmare it had been for us. It wasn't until Art answered most of his questions that he began to realize how close we came to losing our lives. By the time we were halfway home, he began to calm down and asked if there was anything he could do to comfort us.

Art just laughed and said, "Yeah, please don't turn the car heater off. I still have a chill. How about you Dave?"

I smiled and jokingly said, "If you want, I'll close my window." I couldn't believe we could laugh after all we just went through.

Fred was a wonderful father-in-law. He always treated me and his other son-in-law Bill like we were his own sons. I loved him for that.

Barbara was trying to get a commitment out of me. Every chance she got she looked at me and said, "Promise me this is the end – no more!"

I looked at her and said "I love you," which only made her try harder.

Fred continued to ask question after question and, as I was answering them, I realized that Barbara was starting to ask a lot of questions. Suddenly, she broke into tears and uncontrollable sobs.

"What's wrong," I asked.

188

Fred proceeded to tell me that everyone, except himself, was under the impression that the boat went down at 7:17 that evening.

He said, "When I called the Coast Guard back, I got all the information they had. I realized Barb didn't know, after talking to her on the phone, and made the decision not to tell her. When she talked to the Coast Guard station, they told her only that they received a 'May Day' call at 7:17. She called the Ocean City Police, who went to Duffy's house and reported back to her that the boat was not in the dock and Dave's truck was still there."

"I thought it would be the best thing to do at the time. Everyone thought that you had been in the water for five hours, not eighteen. I have to tell you, I was preparing myself for the worst."

"Now, I want to know everything," said Fred, with a tone of excitement in his voice.

"Not now," I said, as I tried to comfort Barb; she was very upset.

"I'm actually glad it worked out that way," I said. "I don't know what you would have done if you had known about it all day." I couldn't wait to get home.

ART

There was talk of keeping us in the hospital overnight, what was left of it, for observation. But we would have none of that. We all wanted to just go home and see our loved ones. They did insist we stay for another hour or so to make sure our core temperatures were rising.

Finally, we could leave. I hitched a ride with Barb, Dave and his father-in-law, Fred, since we lived not too far apart in the same town. Anna was home with Joey, and Fred graciously drove down to retrieve our sorry, soggy asses. The entire trip home, we talked about all that had happened and how tired, hungry and thirsty we were. Fred, being a fisherman, too, wanted to know every detail.

When we pulled into my driveway, Anna was waiting outside on the deck for me. As I struggled to get out of the car, she came over to me and we kissed and hugged and just held each other for a minute before waving to Dave and Barb and Fred as they pulled out of the driveway. It was the best kind of hug; the kind where you both realize you almost lost each other forever. There we were, swaying slowly, hugging in our driveway, with tears rolling down our faces, thankful to still be together. Finally, I said, "I have to see Joey."

I hobbled upstairs to his room where he was sound asleep in his crib. I scooped up my son and held him close, looking at his innocent sleeping face and thinking how fragile life is, and how close he came to growing up fatherless. I couldn't take my eyes off him. More tears. After awhile, Anna came in and put her arms around both of us and said, "This is as it should be."

Ever since, I have looked at every year, month, day, hour and minute as a bonus – a second chance that I nearly didn't get.

I finally put Joey gently back into his crib, thankful he had slept through the whole ordeal. I looked at Anna and told her that I just had to get some sleep. I felt as though I was in a daze and that this was all a dream. I crawled into bed and was instantly asleep for the next eighteen hours.

DAVE

We pulled up in front of our house and Lee, my mother-in-law, came quickly from the house. She looked at me as I was getting out of the car and said, "Oh, thank God." I was then almost knocked back into the car by the kids, who were right behind Lee.

They were crying because they heard their mother crying, which started me crying, which then started Fred and Lee crying.

"Call your mother and father right now," insisted Lee.

I said in a clear voice, "Okay. Let's all go in now. I'm alright and there's no need to sit out here and cry all night."

As soon as I got in the house, I called my mother and father. The phone didn't get a full ring in before it was answered.

"Hi, Mom," I said and all that came back was, "Oh, David," and silence. I assured her that I was fine and everything was alright and then she handed the phone to my father. I was sure what kind of response I was going to get when I talked to my mom, but had no idea of how my father was going to react. To be truthful, I was a little nervous about it. I must say I was relieved when he asked if he could do anything and, after me assuring him that there wasn't anything, told me to get to bed and get some rest.

I hung up the phone and suddenly felt incredibly tired. Sleep was overtaking me. After I announced that I was going to lie down, I found myself surrounded by my children. On my way to the bedroom, they would run ahead of me, anticipating my every move and doing it for me, then return to my side, one of them being with me at all times. Lisa ran ahead and turned the hall light on, then Laura left me long enough to open the bedroom door. Lisa left me long enough to get the bedroom light on as Barbara and her parents followed us in. Lynn, the youngest, never left my side. Once inside the bedroom, I hit the sheets and didn't wake up until the next morning. I had no idea what time it was when I went to sleep, but I remember waking up the next morning and wondering if it was all real. I was headed out to the kitchen in my bathrobe and pajamas.

As I got to the dining room, I met Barb, who said upon seeing me, "Get back in bed."

"Why?" I said. "I'd sooner sit or lie down on the couch."

"How about some tea, then?" she asked, knowing that I would ask for coffee. I gave her a quick look.

"You drink too much coffee," she responded. "But if it's coffee you want, you got it." As she started to set up the coffee pot, she said, "I didn't send the kids to school today," which was a statement that needed no further explanation. Next, she said, "And, if the phone doesn't stop ringing, I'm pulling it off the wall. Also, if you feel up to it, you should call your brothers and sisters."

"I will, a little later," I said and, as we spoke, I realized we were not getting any phone calls.

She looked at me and said, "I know. I took the phone off the hook. I had to; it started at five-thirty this morning. Everyone is concerned, and I know they mean well. It's just that I can't get off the phone. It just rings again the minute I put it down. I called your mom and mine and told them I was taking it off the hook. I also called Linda and asked her to call the other women in the prayer chain to let them know everyone was safe and to thank them. Your mom said that your brothers are on their way over to see you."

I was really sore and tired, but I didn't feel like sleeping. Barb came in to the living room with pillows, sheets and a blanket in her arms and said, "If you want to stay out here, that's fine, but I don't want you off the couch."

I laughed and asked, "What happens if I feel better after school?"

I lay back on the well-made bed my wife had just put together for me and said, "Happy Birthday, Dear." Then I said again, "I'm sorry about all this."

She dropped everything she was doing and came to the side of the couch to assure me she was fine and thought my being here and alive was the best gift she could ever hope for. So I asked her if she would like the same thing next year. With that, she jokingly slapped my shoulder and called me a bum as she headed into the kitchen. She returned with two cups of coffee.

As she sat down, I asked who all the calls were from and she began to tell me. Some of them were people I had worked for and others were friends, aunts and uncles, but they just called to check on my condition. They all understood what was going on and would hang up as soon as she told them I was doing okay.

"You are doing okay, aren't you?" she asked.

"I feel fine. Maybe you ought to put the phone back on, I don't mind."

"Well, now that you're up, I might, but I'm not letting you talk to anyone; you need the rest."

As Barb got up to put the phone back on, our dog came into the room and laid her head by my hand. As I pet her head, I began to feel the need to shower everyone with affection. I don't know what it was, but I had to be with the people and the things I loved. I wanted to hug my wife and kids and just be around the house. I can't explain the feeling, but didn't seem to mind it at all. I looked out the back window from where I was sitting and loved my back yard. I felt like I didn't have a care in the world and turned my head to look at the dining room, and I loved it.

Then the phone rang and Barb answered and said, "Yes. Yes. No. He's fine, just resting. Thank you for calling. I'll tell him you called."

As she hung up the phone, she said, "Are you sure you want it on? That was the lumber yard asking if you're alright."

"How about that?" I laughed. "Did they ask about my account?"

Barbara answered, "No, it was just to see how you were feeling. Everyone really is concerned about you."

All of a sudden, I loved the lumber yard and I wanted Barb to come over next to me because I wanted to love her. I couldn't control the feelings and all I wanted to do was tell everyone I loved them and to hug them.

As Barb half laid down next to me on the couch, the doorbell rang and she said, "I hope this is your brother. I don't think I can handle company right now."

It was two of my brothers, Vincent, the oldest, and Ed, the next to the oldest. Before they could get to the den where I was, I was up and standing. Both brothers had just said hi to Barb, who was on her way to answer the phone. As they entered the den, I hugged both of them and kissed them. I'm sure they thought I was over-reacting to their visit, but I really felt compelled to do it. They both sort of backed away from me, saying, "How you feeling?"

We have always been a close family, especially in times of trouble, but I can honestly say I can't remember the last time I kissed my brothers. I tried to explain to them that I was in a loving mood and that I couldn't stop myself from expressing it.

Before I could, my brother Vince cracked a joke to help me and them relax. He asked me, "What kind of guys did you go fishing with anyway?" I knew right away that he meant no offense and laughed.

The next question was, "What happened out there?" I knew that he was now serious, so we all sat down and, in about five minutes, I gave them a brief rundown. Knowing that they were just there for a short visit, I covered just the important parts of the previous night and told them I would share the whole story with them later.

As they got up to leave, after asking if they could do anything for me, they both came over to me and kissed me and hugged me, saying, "Just call if you need us." I have never in my life had to ask for help, but always knew that if I needed help I could call on any one of my family members. This was the way my mother and father brought us up. There was never a lack of love in our house and I can only thank my parents for that. As my bothers headed for the door, my brother Eddie called back and said Stan, my other brother, would be here after work.

Barb then turned to me and said, "Guess who called while you were with your brothers?"

I laughed and said, "That's not a fair question."

"Channel Ten News – they want to interview you for the news."

This really hit me and I said, "Why me?"

She told me that none of the other guys wanted to be interviewed and all they get at Duffy's is an answering machine. I had never talked on television before and the first thought of it scared me, so I said no without thinking about it.

"Okay. I don't think it is a good idea either," as she picked up the phone and started dialing a number.

I said, "What are you doing?"

She said, "They asked me to call them back with your answer."

"Wait a minute," I said and she pressed down the receiver.

"You don't need the pressure and, besides, you haven't rested since you got up."

"When did they want to do this?" I asked.

"He didn't say, but why would you even consider it anyway?"

"Just for the simple reason that I'm here, and I believe I wouldn't be if it weren't for the Lord. I really believe that the Lord saved us out there. So, if they will let me thank Him in the interview, I'll do it."

After that statement, Barb stopped asking me to reconsider and asked what I wanted her to tell the newsmen when she called them back.

"Just tell them that I'll agree to an interview if they'll agree to let me give thanks to the Lord for saving my life."

Barb thought for a moment and then dialed the number. In a second, someone on the other end answered and Barb asked for the person who had left the message with her.

In less than a minute, Barb was talking to someone and, as I listened, I heard her say, "Yes, he would, but on one condition."

After hearing the condition, she broke into a smile and said, "Good. What time would you be coming by."

Her smile turned into a blank face and she said, "What?" as she turned and looked at me, then repeated "twenty minutes". I just looked back at her. She then spoke into the phone and said, "Fine. Try to give me a few more minutes, okay? Goodbye."

As she hung up the phone, I could see that I just lost contact with my wife, who was surveying the kitchen and den from the dining room.

"They're coming here in twenty minutes and look at this house!"

Just then, my oldest daughter Lisa appeared and my wife said, "I've still got to dress the kids."

I got to witness one of the fastest house-cleanings that has ever been reported. During this time, she answered the phone, which rang every two minutes like clockwork.

I asked what I could do and she said, "Take a shower and put the clothes on I lay out for you."

This was the first time I could ever remember not looking forward to a shower. As I went into the bedroom and started getting ready, I noticed a large orange stain on my right thigh. At first I thought it was a bruise, but soon realized it was from my key chain that had been in my pocket all night. My key chain and keys had turned into a lump of rust, which left a stain on my thigh. It was the first thing I tried to get off once I got in the shower. I tried to take a hot shower, but I found that I had developed sores all over my body from the salt water and where my clothes had rubbed against me. I must say that I felt a lot better after my shower.

As I was getting dressed, Barb came in the room and put some real pressure on me when she said, "Have you thought about what you're going to say to these people? You do know that they're going to be here in just a few minutes?"

Behind her was my youngest daughter Lynn and all she was after was a hug, which I gave her.

"Well?" said Barb, knowing that she was sensing my nervousness about her first question.

"No, I don't and I'm really wishing I hadn't said anything now."

Her next words were very encouraging as she said, "The Lord pulled you out of the ocean. I'm sure He's not going to walk away from you during an interview."

"You're right," I said. Boy, was I glad to have that thought to think on as I left the bedroom. All three of my daughters were in the living room waiting for me and, as I entered, they started bombarding me with questions like, "Do you know you're going to be on TV?" and "Will we be able to see you?"

Before I could answer one of the questions, Barb asked the girls if anyone had asked Dad how he was feeling and that helped calm down the level of excitement that they had gotten themselves into.

As we headed for the den, the phone rang and all three kids made a beeline for it, but stopped short of it as Barb yelled, "Don't answer it." As she walked past the kids, she said, "Not until I tell you what I want you to say when you answer it." As she picked up the phone and said, "Hello," her voice broke into another warm 'hello' followed by a smile as she looked at me and said, "It's your sister, Tina."

Tina was calling from California where she has lived for the last six years. Talking to her, I explained a little of what happened and also how glad I was to hear from her, assuring her I was fine. As we talked, I heard the doorbell ring and Barb said, "Guess who's here? Right on time, too."

It was hard to believe only twenty minutes had passed since making plans for the interview. I explained to my sister what was going on and asked if she would mind if I called her back later. She agreed after I promised to call her back.

Before I could hang up the phone, three guys passed me, half-turning so as not to bump into me. I watched them starting to set up small tripods and one guy was holding a little box that looked like a transistor radio. He was turning in circles, saying, "More light; there's just not enough light in here."

When I suggested opening the curtains, a voice came from behind me, "Don't worry about them. They're with me and they'll handle all that stuff. If it would be possible for us to sit down, I'd like to go over a few things before we start."

I remembered how nervous I was, but all this going on didn't really bother me because it was all happening so fast, I guess. Heading into the den, which is where all the action was taking place, a very concerned and very nice news announcer introduced himself to Barb and me as Brian Williams with *CBS News*.

It was amazing how, with all the commotion, he was able to go directly to what he wanted us to do, what he was going to do and how he was concerned over my condition. To be honest, he was very good at calming me and organizing what was going on. He had a prepared list of questions that he went over with me and, as I listened to him, I realized all the noise in the background had stopped. Turning, I saw two cameras and a few lights at different locations.

"Anytime you're ready, Brian," was a reply from the guy who was worried about the light earlier.

"Try to be yourself and feel free to say anything you want."

As promised, at the end of the interview, I was given a chance to thank the Lord for saving us and I felt really good about that. As fast as the television crew organized and set up, they were twice as fast at breaking down and leaving. I don't think they were there fifteen minutes and, as they were heading for the door, we asked the announcer what time it would be on.

"More than likely, at six o'clock," he said. "Unless something big starts up. If not, it will definitely make the eleven o'clock news."

I walked Brian to the front door, which was still open and another face appeared, looking in through the screen door.

Opening the door to let Brian out, the man introduced himself, "Hi, I'm Don with *The Press of Atlantic City.* I'd like to ask you a few questions about your fishing trip if you're up to it."

I let out a half of a laugh, looked at Barb and said, "Sure, come on in." I offered Don a cup of coffee and before I knew it we were forty-five minutes into an interview. Don asked if he could get a picture of us as a family. He then picked up his stuff, thanked us for our time and headed out. As I shut the door behind him, I felt a wave of calm come over the house.

My daughter Laura started asking if they could stay up and watch, as Lisa tuned in with "Can I call my friends?"

Barb answered Laura's question first with, "We'll see how you behave," and Lisa next with, "All your friends are in school."

It was only ten-thirty in the morning and already I felt tired, and I was starting to feel stiff. I couldn't believe I was getting so tired so fast. I had felt great after I got out of the shower and during the interview.

Barb looked at me and, with just one glance, said, "Okay. That's it. You're done – bed or couch. Those are the only choices you have."

"Couch," I said, while weaving my way toward the den.

Barb, who was just starting to relax after all the excitement, was following me. Passing the kitchen, the phone rang and she said, "And I'm taking it off the hook, like it or not."

I answered, "I like it," and headed for the couch. She headed for the kitchen phone.

I got myself comfortable and I noticed that Barb had appeared in the doorway to the kitchen. I watched her determined look melt and she said, "Alright, hold on for a second." She then put her hand over the mouthpiece of the phone and said, "There's a friend of yours from high school on the phone. He sounds so sincere and concerned about you. Do you want to talk to him or just call him back? His name is Howard and he said you'd remember him."

Recalling high school friends and the few Howards I knew who could talk their way past Barb, I drew a blank and said more out of curiosity, "I'll take the call."

She walked toward me and said, "After this, it's off the hook," and then sort of apologized for letting this call through. She said again, "He's really concerned and I thought that was nice."

I took the phone and said, "Hello" as if I knew who the Howard on the other end was.

"Dave, thank God, you're alright," was what came back.

I still had no idea who I was talking to. Before I could figure out who it was, the voice continued and didn't stop talking from the minute I got the phone. He was talking so loud he could be heard by Barb who was standing just a few feet away.

The next statement he made was, "If I knew you were out there, I would have been out there looking for you in my boat."

This really put the pressure on me. "Now, who is this?" I thought. I was now convinced that I would never remember, so gave up and said, "I'm sorry, Howard, but I just can't place you in my mind." I doubted my own memory now.

"It's me!" he almost yelled back. "Howard Haden. I just heard about your accident."

Still confused, I started to feel a little ashamed of myself because I knew Howard in high school, but never really hung around him and didn't know if I would even call him if something like this happened to him. Well, anyway, the ice was broken and I could now talk to him a lot easier, now that I knew who he was. He began to ask questions about the trip and where we went down. When he started to lose me with the questions he was asking, I stopped him and started asking him a few questions of my own.

"So, what are you doing these days?"

This was the first time I heard silence on the line and just as I was about to ask if he was still there, he came back with an almost-salesman-like-pitch.

"I'm in the salvage business, didn't you know? Well, you know... if you wanted... we could locate and re-float the boat."

I was suddenly hit with the reality of the call and felt like I had just been had. I pulled the covers off and started to stand up.

Seeing the look on my face, Barb said, "What's wrong?"

I motioned to her with my hands that everything was okay and started walking to the kitchen to hang up the phone. Howard, who sort of suspected that was what I was doing, asked as many questions as he could, as fast as he could, only to have me say, "Look, I got to go, Howard. It was good talking to you. Call Duffy. It's his boat."

"I did," he said. "All I get is his answering machine."

"Oh, well, take care, Howard. See ya." I hung up the phone.

Barb, who was very concerned, asked, "What was that all about?"

I laughed and told her that it was Howard Haden from high school.

"Why did you hang up on him like that?" she asked, still puzzled.

"He was trying to get some information about the boat and where we went down."

"Why?" asked Barb.

"He has a salvage business and was interested in getting the contract to retrieve the boat."

"What? Are you kidding?" she said. "Why, that 'No Good'. He lied to me!"

I couldn't help but laugh as I headed back to the couch. I don't think the President of the United States could have gotten through to me after that call.

Barb then turned to the kids and said, "Daddy's going to take a nap. Let's leave him alone."

I lay back on the couch wondering if I could sleep after getting that phone call. The next thing I knew it was four o'clock. I sat up on the edge of the couch and heard voices in there. I didn't feel like standing up yet and didn't know who was in the kitchen. I also hated the idea of walking around in my pajamas in front of anyone other than Barb and the kids, so I just let out a 'Hello' and was relieved when I saw my brother Stanley's head come around the corner. My brother Stanley and I were only a year apart in age, and were the best of friends.

"I got off work early just to come and see you. And you're sleeping!"

I loved the way my brother never took anything in life seriously, and just seeing him made me feel better. He came into the den and sat on the coffee table across from me and asked how I was doing. As we talked about the trip, I remembered about the phone call from Howard and shared it with him, because I knew he'd remember Howard. We laughed.

After hearing my side of the story, Stanley then turned to Barb and said, "Just what was it that Howard said to you?"

Barb was still upset over how he got her to put me on the phone and just said, "If I ever meet Howard, I'm going to let him know just how I feel about it."

Just then the doorbell rang and Barb went to answer it. Stan asked if it had been like that all day, meaning the phone and the doorbell. I asked if Barb had told him about the news people and he nodded his head.

"Listen," he said. "In about a week, I'll be back and we'll have a beer. I want to hear everything." With that, he stood up and added, "Call if you need anything."

Just as he turned around to go, my two other sisters Monica and Marie appeared, both holding pots.

"We thought you'd be hungry and we knew you were all tired, so we brought dinner over. We're just going to drop it off and leave." Both sisters were upset and I didn't want them to just say 'Hi' and leave, so I called them in just to assure them that I was alright.

Stan said, "Boy, you're lucky you didn't go down today. It's really nasty out there."

I hadn't really noticed the weather at all. Then Stan turned and said, "See you later."

When my two sisters came back from putting their pots of food in the kitchen, they just looked at me and started to cry. This really touched me since I knew how much they cared for me. As I tried to stop my own tears, Monica said, "You better never go fishing again," almost in a scolding voice. Marie said, "You're all swollen. Oh, David, please don't do this ever again."

I laughed and said, "Okay, I won't. It wasn't as much fun as I thought it would be anyway!"

I could see that they were beginning to get over being upset as Barb entered the room with reddened eyes. I could see what got them started with the tears.

Once Barb sat down, Marie mentioned, "You really are going to give up canyon fishing, aren't you?"

Almost at once, I could feel a conspiracy that had been put together in the other room starting to form. I looked for my only ally, who had just shut the front door on his way out.

"I probably will for this year," I said with a laugh, which did not bring a smile from any one of the ladies. Monica asked if they had given us anything for the sores we had on our ankles.

As I started to answer her questions, Barb tuned in by saying, "What do you mean...'not this season'? Haven't you learned your lesson?"

I could see I was outnumbered and only a fool would continue to fight or even try to argue with this group. So I said, "Well, the way I feel now, I don't think I will be doing any deep-sea fishing for awhile."

This seemed to calm them down and I went back to my sister's question about my ankles. "No, they didn't, but I think I'm going to put something on them because they're starting to dry out and hurt now."

This statement brought sympathy from all the girls and I knew that they were going to stop asking about my fishing venture. I was glad they stopped by. It's very comforting to have a family that means this much to you at a time like this.

The kids, who had been better than average, as far as behavior goes, were watching from a distance throughout the day at the events that were going on. After my sisters left, I called them all in and explained that soon this commotion would be over, thinking that they might be getting upset about everything that was going on. I was surprised to find out that they were not the least bit upset, but were kind of enjoying the unusual action and were very touched by the way everyone was treating us.

I was feeling rested and I was sure the nap I took had something to do with it. After dinner, Barb asked if there was anything she could do for me. I asked if she had heard from Joe, Art, Dwayne or Duffy. She hadn't, so I said I would like to call to see how they felt. I called Joe first; his wife answered and said Joe was doing fine, but he was lying down right now. She was very thankful that I called. Then she added that Joe had her drive him to work around ten-thirty and pick him up at three o'clock. He'd been sleeping since he got home.

I couldn't believe it. I told Janet, "He's a better man than me. I think I would have died if I had gone to work today."

She said, "Getting upset with him didn't help and, considering what you guys went through, I felt it was better to just let him do his thing." She then said that Joe had been asked to share his story at the Lions Club meeting this week. I asked Janet to have Joe give me a call when he was feeling up to it and she promised to do so.

After hanging up, I shared Joe's wife's story with Barb..., about Joe going to work. Barb said, "If you think going to work was any easier than answering all the phone calls, doing the television interview and handling *The Press* reporter who showed up at the door... then I don't know what to say."

Next, I called Duffy and got what everyone else got... the answering machine. I left a short message that basically asked how he was doing and, if he felt up to it, to call me. Then I called Dwayne; his wife answered and said he wasn't talking to anyone. Without pushing, I asked if there was anything I could do for him, or if he felt up to it, to have him give me a call. I called Art last because I knew I would talk to him the most. I called twice and got a busy signal and was about to give up, thinking he had the phone off the hook. When the third call went through, I was glad because I really felt like talking to Art. I was a little surprised to hear his voice answer the phone.

"I was going to call you," said Art, who sounded good... or, that is to say, normal, over the phone.

"How you feeling?" he asked.

"I'm sorer than ever and a little stiff but, other than that, I'm not doing too bad. I was wondering how the other guys were doing." With that said, I filled him in on the phone calls I had made to them.

"I can't wait to hear how you guys made out," I said to Art.

He replied, "If you're feeling up to it, why don't you and Barb and the kids stop by and we'll fill each other in on what went on after we left each other."

"I was hoping we could do that," I said. "I'm a little tired of sitting in the house."

CHAPTER TEN

I couldn't wait to hear Art's story or, for that matter, tell him about our night. I can't explain the excitement I felt. It wasn't for the fun of it; I think it was a way of convincing myself that it really was over, or maybe it was just about being able to talk to someone who I knew would understand me.

Art asked if we would mind coming to his house. He explained how much preparation was needed to take his son Joey out; he was still only twenty-one months old.

I asked Art to hold on while I ran it by Barb.

She said, "That depends, how do you feel?"

"I'm fine. I'd like to go there, just to get out of the house a little."

"As long as you feel up to it. It would be good to get out a little after all the phone calls and company we've had today," she said.

I turned my attention back to the phone as Barb called to the girls to get ready. I told Art that we would be there in about a half-hour or so.

As I hung up the phone and turned around, something happened. I can't really explain it. I guess it's just one of the love moments I had earlier. I looked at my wife, who was filling the girls in on our plans, when I suddenly saw the woman who had caused me to drop a bucket of eels.

I walked over and gently touched her shoulder, only to have her turn and face me. "What's wrong?" she asked.

As our eyes met. I said, "Nothing. I'm just worried about you and how you're doing." For a moment, we just stared at each other. I was hoping she was looking at that carpenter.

Suddenly tears started forming in both of our eyes and we embraced each other. Within a minute, we had three little girls gathered around our legs.

"I'm fine," Barb said, after a few minutes of regaining her composure. "It will be good to get out of the house for awhile."

As I stepped out of the house and felt the fresh air hit my face, I remembered how the air had felt on my face the night before. I asked my oldest daughter, Lisa, to go back into the house and get me a sweater. Barb seemed upset when I did this because it wasn't that cold out.

"Are you still cold?" she asked.

"No, but if I get a chill I want to have it." I was always known for hardly ever getting cold, so asking for a sweater was really something different.

As I started walking toward the car, I began to walk a little differently and Barb again asked if I was well enough to go. I didn't think getting to the car was going to be a problem, but it turned out to be a real task.

"Yeah, I'm trying not to aggravate the sores on my legs."

There was never a doubt in my mind that she would ever let me drive, so I headed for the passenger side where Lynn and Laura were waiting for me with the door open wide. As I stiff-legged my way into the car, the girls asked with very concerned voices if I was all right. I assured them that I was.

As the sound of the car's engine reached my ears, I turned and looked at the house and remembered pulling away just two nights ago. I started realizing just how blessed I was to still be alive. I couldn't stop looking at the house as we pulled away.

As we pulled up at Art's, I asked Barb what time it was. I still could not keep a wristwatch on because of the swelling all over my body.

"Five-forty-five," was her reply.

"Well, pretty soon we'll know if we made the news or not."

As we made our way up the sidewalk and onto the porch, the door was opened before we got within knocking distance. Anna was standing in the doorway and smiling. As we got to the door, she said, "I'm really glad to see you."

ART

I heard Dave and Barbara's car pull up in the driveway and couldn't wait to give a bear hug to one of the luckiest five people in the world. The contrast between floating out in the ocean close to death with no hope of rescue one day, and then being in my own home safe and sound the next was surreal. The fact that we all survived was even more astounding. It was beginning to register with me that it was going to be a long time before we could get some real perspective on the events of the last couple of days and how they might affect the rest of our lives.

By the time Dave got to the door, we both had huge grins on our faces and hugged each other like we hadn't seen each other in twenty years, instead of only twenty-four hours. After Dave, Barb and the kids came in and we all settled down with some coffee and tea, Dave looked over at me and said, "Do you realize how lucky we are?"

"I'm just beginning to get a grip on it, Dave. I think it's going to be a long time before I get any kind of real perspective on it. You know, by all rights we should still be floating around out there, don't you?"

"Yeah, Art, too many things had to fall into place for us to be rescued, but somehow it worked out. Thank God for that."

"Amen," I said. "I am just so thankful to be home with my family again."

BARB

" I thought you guys went in the water at 7:30 PM, not 7:30 in the morning. My father knew, but decided to keep that bit of information from me. If I had known that, I would have had a nervous breakdown by the end of the day for sure."

"Sunday morning, I had Dave's lunch in the fridge, the coffee maker all set up and ready to go, a kiss goodbye and a wish for good luck to catch plenty of fish...and also a prayer for his safety. I got up around 7:30, had coffee and then woke up Lisa, Laura and Lynn so we could get ready for church. When we came home, we went for a bike ride down the bike path. On the way home, we decided to stop by my friend Cyndy's house for a visit, which soon turned into an invitation for dinner. I knew Dave wouldn't be home until later, so we stayed and had a delightful time. We even joked about what time Dave would get home, especially if they were catching fish. We left Cyndy's house around seven in the evening and came home to get the girls ready for bed, since they had school the next day."

Barb continued. "By this time, I was thinking that I should have had a phone call from Dave. I knew it was time for him to be returning home, but I also knew that if the fish were biting, he wouldn't head in until the bitter end. So I busied myself with getting the girls ready for bed and pushed thoughts of Dave to the back of my mind. Sometime around 9:00 PM, I really started worrying about not getting a phone call from him. He would always call me when he got back to the dock, knowing that I worry until I hear that he is home safe. Because of this, I knew that Dave was not back in yet."

" By 9:30, I called my father, the man that taught Dave to love deep sea fishing. Dad was concerned and told me that we should call the Coast Guard, because their boat may have broken down and they may have had to tow the boat back to the dock, which would make them very late."

"I think that's when you first called me," Anna said. "You called to see if by any chance Art had checked in yet. When I said 'no he hadn't', I could hear the change in your voice. I was concerned, too, but I thought they may be just running late. If there's fish to be caught, Art always stays as long as possible, too. When you told me you were going to call the Coast Guard, I started to really worry."

Before Barb could continue , Lisa wandered over and asked if we had the right channel for the news.

"Why?" Anna asked.

"Because we're going to be on the news!" Lisa said with a huge grin.

"You are? How did that happen?" Anna asked.

Dave explained, "Brian Williams, from *Channel 10 News*, called and wanted to do an interview. To tell you the truth, at first I almost said no. But I thought about it and I'm so grateful to be alive, I thought it would be a good time to thank the Lord for saving us."

"Well you're a better man than me," Art said. "I didn't get out of bed until noon and the last thing I felt like doing was an interview. A reporter did stop by from *The Press* and I gave him our story, but he was only here for about twenty minutes. We didn't hear from *Channel 10 News*, but we have been getting calls from people and friends we haven't talked to in ten years. It was nice they cared enough to do that. I even got a call from Howard Haden, who I hardly know, but he was just fishing for information on where the boat went down. Apparently he has a salvage operation. I told him he was out of luck and hung up."

Dave laughed. "Man he didn't waste any time. He called me, too, acting like a long lost friend when all he cared about was the salvage job. I hung up, too, when I understood what he was after."

With that, the six o'clock news came on and we all watched in silence until it was obvious the story wasn't going to be on until the eleven o'clock news. The girls were really disappointed and, in unison, asked if they could stay up late to watch it. Barb and Dave, being very diplomatic, gave the usual parent answer, "If you're good, maybe you can stay up." That made them happy and they scampered off to play with Joey, who was just loving all the attention.

BARB

Barbara returned to her story. "When I picked up the phone to call the Coast Guard, I could barely contain the panic I felt. I have never had to call them before. Dave would always call me at the last minute, apologizing for making me worry saying, "But the fish were biting." This time it was different. It was much later. I hadn't heard from Dave and Anna hadn't heard from Art either. It just didn't feel right. As I prepared to make the call, I began to realize that I didn't know the name of the boat. I didn't know specifically where they were headed, just 'the canyon'. I didn't know the LORAN coordinates. I felt foolish, but I picked up the phone and called them anyway to report them being overdue."

"When I reached the Coast Guard, they informed me that there was no record of a call from Dave, but they did have a 'May Day' that was called in at 7:17. They knew there were five men aboard, but they only had one LORAN coordinate to try to locate

213

them with. He said they had been sweep searching with helicopters, but hadn't found anything yet. He asked me if this sounded like my husband and his crew and I had to admit to them that I didn't know any details about this boat. I knew the boat owner's name and I knew that Dave had invited Joe and Art, but that's all I knew. They asked me to go see if the boat had returned to the dock, but I was in no condition to drive, so I called the Ocean City Police and they were kind enough to confirm that Duffy's boat had indeed not returned. I gave this information to the Coast Guard and they said they would keep me informed."

"I hung up the phone and sat on the bed. I felt numb. I couldn't think past the words the Coast Guard had said... that Dave's boat had gone down at 7:17. At the time, I assumed they meant 7:17 p.m..., not a.m. I just couldn't get myself to think any further about what the possibilities of this could mean. "

"I immediately picked up the phone and called a friend to get you guys on a women's prayer chain. At the time, it was an automatic reaction. I knew that I was helpless, but I also knew that the most powerful thing I could do to help you guys was to call on the power of prayer."

"I was still sitting on my bed with the phone in my lap when the Coast Guard called back to confirm that the Mayday was from you guys and that you had been in the water since 7:17. Again, they didn't mention whether it was a.m. or p.m., so I assumed it was p.m. I wondered how cold the water was in September and how long a person could survive. I tried not to let myself think of the details."

"I called my father back and relayed to him what the Coast Guard had said. I hung up the phone and I just sat on the bed and rocked back and forth. I felt so helpless because there was nothing I could do to change the situation, just wait. I called Anna and told her their boat went down and so far they hadn't found anybody. Then I sat there, numb, for about an hour before the phone rang again. It was the Coast Guard. This time they called to tell me that three of you guys had been picked up by a freighter and two were still missing and that they were sending a helicopter to search the area, but they didn't say who had been rescued. I was terrified to think that two were still missing. I called Anna again and told her what I had learned, then I waited and prayed until they called back."

"It was the longest two hours I have ever spent, and then the phone finally rang again. The voice on the phone was a very concerned nurse from Burdette Tomlin Hospital in Cape May. She said she was looking into the eyes of Dave Jones, and he would not let them treat him until she called and told me he was fine! The numbness that had a grip on me disappeared in a nanosecond. I guess it's a way our bodies deal with a situation that our brains are just too frightened to cope with. To this day, I'm thankful that I didn't know they were in the water for eighteen hours until after they were rescued."

"I called Anna to tell her that Dave was one of the three picked up, but I didn't know who the other two were and neither did the nurse. I could hear the tension in your voice. At this point, all I wanted to do was get down there and see Dave. I called my mother and father, who came over immediately. Mom stayed to babysit the girls, while Dad drove me to the hospital. It's about a thirty minute drive, but seemed like hours."

"I ran through the emergency room doors and scanned the hallways for any sign of Dave. The nurse who called me came out and took me right over to Dave. I had never been so thankful to see his beautiful warm eyes smile at me as they did at that moment. I could tell he had been through a lot, but his 'never give up' attitude had kept him going."

ANNA

"After I got your last phone call, I had to decide whether or not to call Art's parents," Anna said. "I decided to wait until I had more information ,and I'm glad I did because, at one point, I got the impression there were no survivors. Then you called and said there were three: one was Dave, one was Joe, but you didn't know who the other one was. I was afraid his dad would have had a heart attack. I guess in all the confusion with you guys being separated and all, it wasn't clear who was where for awhile. When I finally did call them, I knew you had all been rescued. Knowing that made it so much easier to make that phone call."

"Babe," Art said to Anna, "When we were on the helicopter after being picked up off the freighter, one of the corpsman asked me if there was anyone they could notify that we were okay and, of course, I gave him your name and phone number. They were pretty busy attending to us and flying the chopper, so maybe they forgot or they heard the wrong number because of the noise. I'm just happy to be here!"

"Well," Anna said. "I just know the Coast Guard never called me to let me know you were okay and I was getting bits and pieces from Barbara as she learned what was happening. When she found out Dave and Joe had been rescued and were at the hospital, Barb still hadn't been told that you, Dwayne and Duffy had been picked up. Naturally I thought the worst and was just trying to hold myself together and praying they would find you. Now, I find out that you were rescued before Dave and Joe and were having a good old time on that freighter drinking hot coffee and eating donuts, while I was having a nervous breakdown. I should knock you out."

ART

With that comment, we all had a good laugh. That this misadventure could have turned out entirely differently was not lost on us. I could see it in all our eyes as we soaked up the laughter and love in the room, realizing our rescue was truly a miracle. I don't think any of us will ever look at life in quite the same way again.

And so the conversation went, back and forth, all of us thankful beyond imagination that we all had made it. We told our wives as much of our misadventure as we could remember in detail and it all came out in a flood of words and emotions; kind of a purging of our souls. We had come so close to death that we had to keep talking about it to convince ourselves we were still here among the living.

CHAPTER ELEVEN

DAVE

As we all said good night and headed for the door, I turned to Art and said, "Thanks again for keeping our position and sending the Coast Guard out for us."

Art smiled and said, "That was a very scary moment for me, because I kept doubting myself. But it worked out and I'm glad. I kept telling myself I wouldn't leave until I was sure you were picked up."

We stepped out and Barbara looked back and asked Art if he would ever go to the canyon again.

He replied, "Only if I have my own EPIRB with me." An EPIRB is a small transmitter that, once you activate it, sends out an SOS and the Coast Guard can track down the exact location by the beeps.

After Art answered Barb's question, he jokingly said, "Boy, wouldn't that be a great Father's Day present?"

Barb just shook her head and said, "You guys are hopeless."

Although I enjoyed hearing Art's side of what had happened, and also felt good about getting out of the house, I was glad to be headed home. By the time we were halfway home, my youngest daughter Lynn was asleep, and I really felt bad waking her up to get her out of the car. I would have normally carried her in, but was in no condition to perform the fatherly act.

Once inside, the girls got into their pajamas and prepared to watch the eleven o'clock news, which had another fifteen minutes until airtime. It was turning into a big family event. The girls were wide awake, even Lynn, and getting ready for the news. Barb made popcorn and everyone sat down to watch.

About three-quarters of the way through the news, our story came on and, I have to say, they did a really good job of covering it. They even had a tape of our 'Mayday' broadcast, which had to have come from the Coast Guard station. As they continued the coverage, I realized that they had edited out quite a bit of our interview. In fact, when it was just about over, they put in the statement that I believed our rescue was an answer to prayer. I remember being a little upset because I agreed to the interview on the condition that they at least let me thank God for saving our lives out there. But they didn't and, now that the news was over, there was nothing I could do about it anyway.

All the girls got to see themselves on television, and that was pretty exciting for them. After the news, I replayed the part of the news that covered our story, and then issued the 'off to bed' order. They obeyed in an orderly manner, seeing how it was way past their bedtime.

After the kids were put to bed, Barb and I prepared for bed as well. As we lay back under the covers, I was hit with the realization of what day it was.

"I forgot all about your birthday," I confessed, feeling guilty.

Barb replied, "I couldn't ask for anything better than having you home safe."

"I'm really sorry. I didn't even get you flowers," I said.

After a few minutes, Barb said, "I know what you can get me for my birthday."

I asked, "What?" before I could even think about the statement she just made.

"Promise me you'll stop running the canyon trips. I don't care about fishing, but the canyon trips are too much."

I had no way of getting out of this conversation, so I put on my defense and said, "Honey, it was an accident and, if anything, I'll get an EPIRB and never go on a trip unless the weather is perfect. But I'm not ready to tell you 'yes' to something I haven't even thought about."

"What's to think about?" she asked. "You were almost killed on this trip."

I answered, "I know. That's why I would like to think about it for a while." On that line, I felt I got to an end in the conversation, so I mentioned that I was too tired to talk anymore and got no argument from Barb, who I knew was tired herself. Although I was exhausted, I had a hard time falling asleep and found myself lying in bed thinking about my defense for Barb, who I knew would press me about not fishing the canyon again. As I lay there, I couldn't help thinking about the trip and all that had happened during it. I knew that it was something I would never forget.

I reached over to touch my wife for no other reason than to comfort myself and assure myself that I was actually there. This might not make sense to a lot of people, but I remember that touch as much as I do the trip. It was the first time since I had been rescued that I thought about any one of my senses. I was at a point where I wanted to enjoy just a simple, everyday thing.

As I put my hand on her shoulder, I could actually feel something that I had never felt before; I moved my hand down her arm and realized how close I had come to losing my life. At the time, it hadn't scared me as much as it did right now. I was more aware of my senses than I had ever been before. It was this simple touching of my wife's shoulder and arm that gave me the fear of dying. It's not like I have ever thought about death before but, just two nights ago, I had to accept it. Now, here I was tonight just appreciating life through a simple touch.

I continued to enjoy this simple rubbing of my wife's arm and could feel my whole body starting to be more aware of my senses than ever before. It was as if someone had removed a layer of wax from my body that had kept me from ever really feeling anything. I could feel a wave of excitement building in me, as a new appreciation of life was coming over me.

As my hand now passed over my wife's forearm and onto her hand, she turned over and asked if I was alright. In turning, she came closer to me, which sent a surge of sensual contact that I would never be able to explain to anyone. As I began to think that I had experienced the highest peak of sensitivity a man could ever have, my eyes met hers and I felt that the same wax had been removed from my eyes. I looked at her like I don't ever remember looking at her before. I was full of what I now know was true feeling. These were feelings that should exist in everyone's life. I knew how lucky I was to be experiencing them.

The thoughts of fear I had earlier were gone, and I felt totally at peace with the moments I was sharing with my wife. I stared at her face and began to realize that she, too, had had the wax removed from her body. As we pulled toward each other, we both experienced the first good thing that had come from the fishing trip experience.

The morning light found us still holding each other in an embrace neither one of us wanted to end. As we lay on the bed, we promised never to let a moment go by where we would not want to feel each other as we did now. Both of us were aware of the precious gift of life, and we lay there wondering how we had let time put a layer of wax over our feelings – not our thoughts, but our feelings.

Our mornings are regimented and as we started our day, I must say I do remember the pace being a little slower. We both showered and dressed and came out of our room to find that the kids were still asleep. We walked from room to room and looked at each child, being as careful as we could not to wake them, pausing to look at each of their sweet sleeping faces.

It was very hard to think about the on-coming day and all that I had to do and deal with. I had lost a lot of time the week before the trip, plus the trip, and now recovery time. It was going to be hard to get everything in my business back in order, to say nothing of getting my family back to normal.

The business still seemed like a job that was getting bigger and bigger all the time. But, for a lot of reasons, I couldn't get myself up for them. I knew that at one point I would have to confront the problems, but I now had a different outlook on them. I was determined to keep the same frame of mind that I woke up with.

I kept Barb company while she put the kids' lunches together, and we discussed our plans of what had to be done during the day. All the while, Barb insisted I take the day off, which I agreed to under the condition that I get some business calls in. As she poured me a cup of coffee with her back to me, she asked if I would wake the kids up. I headed off in the direction of the kids' rooms, thinking to myself, 'Which one should I wake up first?' I was surprised to find that Lisa had already gotten up and was on her way down the hallway to give me a good morning kiss. I hugged her and told her it was time to get moving.

She said to me, "Boy, you look much better today than you did last night."

As I headed down the hallway to Laura and Lynn's room, I stopped by the bathroom to look at myself in the mirror. I flipped on the light and went straight to the mirror, turned and looked into it. I could see that the swelling was just about all gone and my eyes weren't as red any longer. This made me feel even better.

I left the bathroom and entered the girls' room, which was another chance to dwell on how happy I was to be alive. I looked around and thought of how, at one point two days ago, I actually accepted the fact that I was going to die at sea.

I hated to wake our kids by shaking them, so I always stood in the middle of the room and yelled or clapped my hands until they would promise to get up.

As they started to respond to my awakening call, Lisa yelled down the hallway, "You guys! Our picture's in the paper!"

With that, the covers went flying and two girls flew by me like little rockets, yelling, "Let me see! Let me see!"

When I got to the kitchen, Barb was standing there with a big grin and said, "Well, D.J., you made the front page!"

As I came in, I said to the girls, "Boy, I didn't even get a good morning kiss." Lisa began yelling to prove her innocence that she had given me one, and the other two girls began saying they were sorry and rushed back to kiss me.

"Well," I said to Barb, "Are you going to read it to us?"

This brought an unorganized wave of yells asking her to read it out loud, which I knew she had already intended to do. Barb read the story and we all listened. We heard a brief description of the story and a quote from each of us and a picture of each one of us, with our picture being the only family picture.

The story in *The Press* was not expected and, as Barb finished reading it, I said to her, "Now everyone knows about it."

Her reply was, "Well, what do you think having it on TV did for the spreading of the news?"

I said, "Yeah. I know that, but *The Atlantic City Press*! Everyone gets it. I don't think it would be a wise idea to hang around the phones today."

Suddenly, Barb let out a loud, "Oh, my gosh! Look at the time. You girls are going to be late for school!"

Before the girls broke up and headed back for the bedrooms to start getting ready, they had a small argument over who would be allowed to take the paper into school.

"No one will take it in today," was Barb's solution and she ended the sentence with, "Let's get going. We're late."

It felt good to be just hanging around, not worrying about the upcoming workload, which I decided to face tomorrow.

As the kids emerged from their rooms and came into the kitchen to have Mom do their hair and eat a little breakfast, I noticed they each had a puss face on. I asked why they were so sad, knowing all the time that it was about the newspaper settlement.

"Why can't you share?" I said, which brought a look from Barb, who at the time had two rubber bands in her mouth and both hands and a brush in Lynn's hair.

No one answered and, as Barb took the rubber bands out of her mouth, she said, "Does that answer your question?"

I was having a good time and wasn't going to let it go, so I said, "Why not let Lisa have it in the morning, give it to Laura around ten-thirty and then to Lynn around one-thirty?"

Laura stood up and said, "That's not fair. She always gets to go first."

Lynn volunteered to go first, which made Laura turn and just look at Lynn, who didn't really care one way or another and was totally in agreement with any settlement, just as long as they got to take it in to school.

Lisa chimed in and said, "How about I give it to you at recess," and Laura, who wasn't about to give an inch, said, "How about I give it to you?"

With this, Barb slammed the brush down on the counter and said, "I can't believe you girls are arguing over a newspaper when there's your dad, who could have been killed, and you don't care! You just keep arguing over who's getting the newspaper first!"

I thought, in my mind, "Boy! Was that a good way to end an argument!"

The girls, who were struck with guilt, started insisting that the other one take it first - like it had a curse put on it. The argument had turned completely around and, as I looked over at Barb, she smiled and said, "Had to open your big mouth, didn't you?"

As we walked out to the car, Barb insisted on driving. I still felt sore and a little stiff, so I agreed. We headed off toward the school and the girls never once argued out loud but, boy, the looks they gave each other!

We pulled up in front of the school and I was surprised to see the principal, Nancy Robinson, standing out in front with a newspaper under her arm. As we opened the door to let the kids out, she came over to the car and, with a very sincere voice, asked if we were alright, being surprised to see me in the car. What made this a special event is the fact that I know Nancy loves the ocean and walks about four miles along the beach every day just for the mere pleasure of walking by the sea. I could almost feel that same camaraderie that I had with fellow fishermen, because of her love of the seashore.

"You must be a wreck," she said to Barb, who really had gone through the mill over the last four days. She leaned over Barb and said, "I know it's not fair to ask you this question, but I can't help it. Are you still going to go fishing after this?"

I smiled and said in a low voice, "Yes."

"Well, please do it more carefully. We don't want this to happen again."

"Me either," I said.

I thanked her for her concern and, before we could pull away, another of Barb's friends came up and asked how we were doing and mentioned that they had seen us on TV last night. Nancy, who was still standing by, came over and said to Barb, "Get used to the questions. Everyone who dropped their kids off asked about you and Dave."

We finally got time to pull away after making sure the girls got in okay. By the way, Nancy excused the girls for being late that morning. Barb had confessed to her we were late because of their arguing over who was going to take the newspaper in. Nancy had laughed and said, "I'll give them mine." As we pulled away, she said, "Have a good day and God bless," and then added, "He already did!"

"Well, where to?" asked Barb.

"How about if I take you to Smitty's for breakfast?" I asked, knowing all the while she was going to say 'yes'.

Smitty's is a small waterfront restaurant that caters to fishermen and is loved by the locals for its good and cheap breakfasts. The atmosphere is terrible and the only saving grace is that one wall overlooks the bay and boat docks, along with a nice view of the meadows. It must have been our day because, as soon as we walked in, we got a table right next to the wall overlooking the bay.

As we sat down, in one ear, we could hear the squeaking of the rusted pulleys which helped moor the boats that were bobbing in the water and, in the other ear, was the normal restaurant noise that almost, but not quite, drowned out the dock noise. After ordering, we were able to concentrate on each other and on the beautiful view of the bay.

I started our conversation by asking Barb to do me a favor and please stop asking me about big-game fishing and what I was going to do. She said she was sorry for what she had already said and that, after thinking about it, knew that I was the only one who could make that decision. She promised not to pressure me anymore and jokingly said, "But, you know what I want!"

It wasn't until our order came that we happened to notice that half the people in the restaurant were reading the article in the paper about the trip. It was sort of fun to be able to listen to the different opinions and what people were saying about it.

I said to Barb, "I have a feeling that no matter where we go it's going to be like this."

She laughed a little and said, "How about we stop by your mom and dad's for a cup of coffee before someone that knows you comes in?"

We got up and prepared to leave and I took one more look at the bay, still trying to assure myself that pretty soon things would get back to normal. As I paid the lady at the cash register, I asked her what she thought about that boating accident that happened. I did it as a joke and got a real kick out of it when she replied, "They're a bunch of lucky S.O.B.s, if you ask me."

Although I thought her response was funny, I could see that it had upset Barb so, without saying anything more than 'Have a nice day,' I turned and headed for the door with my arm around Barb.

Next stop was my mother and father's house where, if nothing else, we could relax and plan our day. When we got to their house, I was pleased to see a friend of the family's car parked outside.

"Mr. Fox is visiting. Do you still want to stop?" asked Barb.

"Sure," I said, "He's almost like one of the family anyway."

As we entered my mom's kitchen, which is where all company is entertained, she kissed me and said, "I've got about ten papers for you. Don't forget them when you leave."

Barb laughed and said, "Where were you this morning, Mom?" as she explained about the kids wanting to take the paper to school.

My sister Monica was there and, with total sympathy for the kids, said, "You should have stopped on the way and bought them each a paper."

Although her solution would have ended the fighting and was very logical, neither one of us admitted it, which made Monica laugh because she knew she was right.

"Boy, we came here to rest and get grilled by you!" said Barb.

As I looked over, I saw Mr. Fox sitting at the table in front of a cup of coffee and, sensing it was his turn to have a little fun with us, he asked when I would be going fishing again.

I knew better than to try and match wits with him, but always tried anyway. "Why?" I asked. "Would you like to go with me?"

"Well, I don't know. How'd you do the last time you went out?" was his reply.

"Alright, you got me," I said, which was my way of raising the white flag. I really liked Mr. Fox and knew he was just having a little fun, which was one of the reasons I liked him. He always had a way of pulling a laugh out of you.

My dad entered the room, walked by Barb, kissed her on the cheek and said, "I'll be over later with the truck and we'll take all his fishing stuff and throw it out, okay?" This really got a laugh and was exactly what I would have expected my father to say. Both Barb and I were now relaxed.

As I sat down to enjoy a cup of coffee, Mr. Fox asked if I was scared while I was out there. I answered that most of the time I was scared and the rest of the time I was petrified with fear.

"I can't believe it," he said and, in my mind, I figured no one could believe it, because they could have no idea of what it was like. These thoughts were smashed by Mr. Fox's next statement.

"During World War II, I spent three days and three nights in the South Pacific holding on to a rubber raft, waiting for someone in the raft to die so I could have my turn in the raft."

I was overwhelmed by what he had just said and the questions started flowing out of me concerning his ordeal.

"Oh, yeah," he said. "I got two purple hearts for it. I had a chest wound and a hole in my wrist," he said, pulling up his sleeve to show me a very nasty-looking scar on the inside of his wrist.

"My goodness," I said. "This makes my story look like a fairy tale."

"Oh, I didn't tell it to you to downgrade your experience," he said. "I told you so you would know that I really do understand what you went through out there. I'm glad you're alive and sitting here with me," said Mr. Fox.

I had no trouble believing every word he said, and I suddenly felt a little closer to him for no other reason than for his sharing his story with me.

"How come you never told anyone about it?"

"Well, it took me a long time to forget about it; that is to say, the memories are not as clear as they used to be. Someday, I'll bring the medals by and show you."

I went back to playing wits again and asked if he'd give me one of his purple heart medals for the experience that I had.

He replied, "Why, of course, but I have to shoot you first. Where do you want it? In the chest or wrist?"

I turned to Barb and asked, "Where do you think, Hon?"

She smiled and said, "How about the head?"

Before we really got started with all the joking, I said, "Okay. I've got some calls to make and they really can't wait any longer. Thank you for the coffee, Mom and Dad. Mr. Fox, please take care until I see you again."

"I will, David, and you keep dry."

"You never let up, do you?" I yelled, as Barb and I headed out the door.

We headed for the car and I told Barb I would like to drive. She said, "Are you sure you're feeling alright?"

I answered, "I'm feeling fine and, after hearing Mr. Fox's story, I feel even better. How about him?" as I was still thinking about his World War II story. I met someone who knew what my experience was like.

All of a sudden, I started to think back to the night of the rescue and how I couldn't get Barb's dad to understand that the whole ordeal was not a heroic or adventurous thing, and I suddenly realized why Mr. Fox never shared the story with us before. It seems like no matter who I talked to, up to this point, no one really knew how I felt out there with the exception of Mr. Fox. It was a scary, life-threatening ordeal and most people could not understand it, no matter how well I told the story. Not only was this depressing, it was also frustrating to tell the story, only to have them ask if I was now going to give up fishing.

As we pulled up in front of the house, Barb again asked if I was alright.

"Yes. Why?"

"Well, you haven't talked much since we left your mom and dad's house."

"Oh, just thinking," I said.

As we entered the house, I noticed a couple of bouquets of flowers at the other end of the porch. I walked over and picked up the cards, all from concerned friends. Boy, that was very nice of them and I found myself starting to feel like I was going to cry.

Barb, who was now standing next to me, said, "Look, it's been a long morning. Why don't you take a nap?"

"I don't know what's wrong with me. I just can't seem to get a grip on just what I'm doing here. I've got to make those calls," I told her.

Barb, who is always logical, said, "Look, lie down. Take a nap. I'll wake you at three o'clock when I go to pick up the kids. You can stay at home and make your phone calls then."

It was eleven o'clock and I was exhausted and couldn't figure out what had happened to the attitude I woke up with. But the nap was a good idea and I felt like putting my head in the sand anyway. As I got into bed, I felt better almost right away.

Barb came in and said, "See what happens when you overdo? Now go to sleep. I promise to wake you at three o'clock."

It was the first sound sleep I remember having. My body just shut down and, I mean to tell you, I slept. It was three o'clock on the button when Barb came in to shake me and tell me it was time for her to leave to get the kids. I took my time getting out from under the warm covers. I then kissed her goodbye and thanked her again.

I didn't feel like getting dressed, so I threw my bathrobe on and headed for my office, which I really didn't want to do. I sat down and tried to make a list of the phone calls I needed to make, then sat back in my chair and began to just daydream. I turned my head to scan my office and couldn't help but notice the two Penn 6/0 reels and poles standing up in the corner. For a second, I was overcome by greed, or at least that's what I called it, when I started thinking about my two favorite poles and how they were gone. I started to list the things that I had taken along on the trip. I'm going to miss my Old Navy duffel bag. I started to try and remember the contents - and my fishing hat from Montauk. Then I stopped and seriously asked myself if fishing really was worth risking my life for. I reasoned that the whole event had been just an accident.

I got up from my desk and walked over to a wall where I had pictures of previous fishing trips. One, in particular, caught my attention. It was a picture of me standing next to a shark that we had just weighed in, along with a few smaller sharks lying on the dock. Looking at the picture, I started to remember the fears I had of sharks attacking us. It was a strange feeling, knowing I was safe now and thinking how close I had come to becoming part of something I never dreamed could happen.

I began to look at the other pictures, most of which were successful shark fishing trips. I thought to myself, 'I haven't looked at these pictures since I hung them up.' I reached up and took some of them off the wall to get a better look. Staring into the pictures, I remembered each trip and the excitement that I had experienced each time.

I was so caught up in the pictures I didn't realize Barb had returned from picking up the kids, and my daydreams stopped when I heard the front door open and the sound of the girls coming in. I put the pictures down on my desk so I could go greet them. As I met them and received my kisses 'hello', Barb appeared in the door and asked if I got my phone calls finished.

I smiled and said, "I didn't get any of them made."

"Well, that's fine with me," she said. "They can all wait as far as I'm concerned." She walked by and stopped only to give me a peck on the cheek as she headed for the kitchen.

I felt a little uncomfortable being in my bathrobe at four o'clock in the afternoon, so I headed for the bedroom to get dressed. On the way, I heard the phone ring and when I got to the bedroom I could tell it had already been answered. I slipped on a pair of jeans and a tee-shirt. Barb came into the bedroom and said that her mom had just called and invited us over on Saturday for a birthday barbecue for her.

"Sounds great," I said, without a second thought.

"Good!" she said. "I think it will be a lot of fun."

The next day was my first day back to work and the hardest part of the day was telling the story so many times to so many different people. I started to catch up on the workload that I had let build up. I realized I had made plans for Saturday and was looking forward to a day of not having to tell my story.

All week long, I wondered if I would ever feel the same about fishing again. Every free minute I got I tried to think about how much I liked fishing, but I couldn't hold a thought or, for that matter, talk to anyone about fishing without the memories of how I felt out there flooding back to me. I would stop working the minute

I heard a helicopter overhead and every time an ambulance would pass me or even if I just saw a boat, I would have some thought of the trip cross my mind. Near the end of the week, I had myself convinced that fishing would never be the same. I thought about Mr. Fox and wondered how long it took him to get over his fears.

The week finally ended and I found myself lying in bed Saturday morning, exhausted from a sleepless night and wondering what the day would bring. The alarm went off and Barb woke up and clicked it off.

"You know, if you're having trouble sleeping," she said, "I'm sure we could get a prescription that would help you."

"If it doesn't get better soon, I'm going to get something," I said.

I was sitting on the edge of the bed when Barb mentioned, "You didn't forget the birthday party at my mom's, did you?"

"No," I said, "It's three o'clock, right?"

"Yes, but I was thinking of going over early so I could help. Do you mind?"

I really didn't want to go, for no other reason than there was nothing for me to do while all the girls would be in the kitchen and I would probably just sit in the living room and watch TV. But I had no other plans so, if it would make things easier for Barb, I would go.

While the kids were having breakfast and discussing what they were going to do at Grandmom's house, I went out and got the newspaper and returned to the kitchen to have my coffee and a glance at the paper.

"Daddy, we're going to make the birthday cake with Grandmom."

"Sounds like you guys are going to have fun," I said, thinking all the while, 'I hope there's a good football game on or something.'

I opened the paper and couldn't help but go to the sports page to see what the local fishing report had to say. There were no pictures, which meant that it had been a poor week and I could tell by the size of the article that it wasn't worth reading. This all brought the thought of 'who cares about fishing anyway.'

Next, Barb issued an order for the kids to clean up their breakfast dishes and get dressed for Grandmom's and Grandpop's house, which they did. Then she turned to me and said, "You take your shower first while I clean up and then I'll take mine and we'll leave, okay?"

"Sounds good," I said, as I folded up the paper and walked into the living room to put it in the rack. As I bent down to put the paper back, I heard a noise on the front porch that got my attention. It was the sound of the mailbox closing after the mailman, Mr. Ryan, dropped off our mail. I opened the door and yelled 'hello' to him. He just smiled and waved. There didn't seem to be anything but bills and junk mail, so I headed into my office to drop it on my desk.

I got there and was surprised to see the pictures I had taken off the wall still on my desk. I turned my head and glanced at the two Penn 6/0 poles and reels standing in the corner, then started to pick up the pictures and enjoy the memories that went with them. I found myself daydreaming about the fishing trips that produced the pictures. My thoughts all week were if I'd ever have that same desire to fish again like I used to.

My thoughts were broken when I heard an upset voice in the doorway, "You haven't even showered yet. I wanted to get there early and you're standing around doing nothing," said Barb.

I just stood there, defenseless over the fact that I had no excuse other than daydreaming. Just before I tried to explain to her why I hadn't done anything, the phone rang and I picked it up, looking at Barb the whole time.

"Hello?"

The voice that came through said, "Oh, good, you're home. Listen, the 'tog are running like crazy. If you want to go, I'll pick you up in a half hour."

"Hold on," I said, then put my hand over the mouthpiece and asked Barb, who was looking at me with a 'well-who-is-it' look, "What time do we have to be at your mom's?"

"Who is that?" she asked.

"Art"

With that, she dropped both hands to her sides and said, "Do what you want. The girls and I are going to Grandmom's to make the cake. You better be there by three o'clock, or else."

I took my hand off the mouthpiece and said, "I'll be ready." I was going on a fishing trip for 'tog and could feel the excitement building as I tried to remember where my small pole was..., and if I had any crab in the freezer for bait.

THE END

EPILOG

DAVE

A lot of time has passed since our ordeal. People often ask me if there's anything I would have done differently, if I could. I always laugh and say, "Yes, I would have gone to church instead of fishing."

The truth is, I don't have any regrets. I'm thankful things turned out the way they did; by that, I mean everyone made it back without any serious injuries. I believe I'm alive and well today because of my Lord and Savior, Jesus Christ. He answered our prayers and taught me the true meaning of dependence.

I have always been able to fix or handle any problem or situation I found myself in. I liked to think... or that is to say, I always felt capable of dealing with anything that happened to me. During our trial at sea, I experienced total helplessness for the first time in my life. It was something, at the time, I believed I would never forget and I was very thankful. It's funny how life just continues on. I thought I would never forget about that feeling of being totally helpless. I could not tell the fishing story without crying at some point; I was so thankful.

But, in today's times and in the everyday hustle, memories are sometimes clouded over. Three years ago, my youngest son broke his neck diving into a pool at a friend's house. My wife and I spent six hours praying in his hospital room, while two floors below us a team of doctors were operating on my son. This time we both experienced that feeling of being totally helpless.

This year, I watched my son play goalie on his school's soccer team. Now I can't tell his story without crying. I have learned (I hope) never to let life's problems cloud my mind or memory.

I have met Duffy about a half dozen times since the boating accident. He has been very standoffish, and does whatever he can to end our conversation as quickly as possible. He wouldn't even participate in the reenactment that was produced by *Outdoor Life Network*. I met Dwayne once since then, and he acted pretty much like Duffy did - no return phone calls or communications at all.

Art and I are still the best of friends, fishing and clamming whenever we get the chance. The last time I saw Joe was during the reenactment. It was a lot of fun and we all had a good time. Joe is retired now, but whenever we see each other it always ends with smiles and hugs. I worked with Joe's daughter for awhile. She shared with me that Joe spends most of his time being the best grandpa he can be to all of his grandchildren. She shared a story of Joe sitting in a little blow-up kiddie pool in his back yard with the youngest grandchild. I had no problem picturing Joe in that pool and knowing he was enjoying every minute of it.

I am thankful to the crew of the *Melvin H. Baker* and will always be indebted to the brave men and women of the United States Coast Guard for our rescue. But above all, I am thankful to my Lord and Savior, Jesus Christ for answering our prayers.

Daniel David Jones

Proverbs 3:5-6 *Trust in the Lord with all your heart, and lean not upon your own understanding. In all your ways, acknowledge Him and He will direct your path.*

ART

Any one of us, under enough pressure, desperation or torture, will do things we normally wouldn't do. It is this premise that allows me, in my heart, to forgive Dwayne and Duffy for drinking those last two sodas, oblivious to the fact that their actions could have killed the rest of us, denying us sustenance that could have lengthened our lives long enough to be rescued. What I don't understand are their actions, or lack of them, following our rescue. They never made an attempt to make it right, apologize, or in any way face what they did. When Dave ran into them later on, neither of them could look him in the eye. Maybe they got a good view of what they were made of and didn't like what they saw. Facing almost certain death can change people, but I guess not everyone reacts positively.

When I was seventeen years old, driving to my summer job, I experienced another near-death event of a different kind. My buddy, Randy, and I were traveling the back roads of South Jersey on our way to work cleaning area swimming pools. I was not familiar with the back roads and ran a stop sign, which was covered by a tree branch. In the next split second, we crossed a busy intersection at virtually the same time that a fully loaded dump truck crossed in front of us. After passing through the intersection, unscathed and coasting to a stop on the shoulder of the road, our reaction was, "Holy shit! What just happened?" Our response, as the reality of what had almost happened sunk in and adrenalin coursed through our bodies, was nervous laughter.

Frozen in my brain is the image of the side of that truck, inches from the hood of my car, uncannily similar to the side of the *Melvin H. Baker*, including the rust stains and rivets. The difference being the dirt and gravel hitting my hood and windshield as opposed to water hitting my face and the incredible speed with which this happened – it happened in a blink of an eye compared to eighteen hours of struggling to survive. Had we arrived at the intersection a split second sooner, we would have been road kill, no doubt.

Comparing these two experiences made me think... if I had the choice, which way would I choose to enter the next life? Would it be quickly, not having the time to say goodbye or think about my life... or with some time to sort things out and say goodbye? They each have their advantages. Go quickly and there is no suffering, no time to panic, be scared or deal with regrets. Pass slowly and you have time to peruse your life, say goodbye and deal with any regrets. Either way, none of us get out of here alive.

The truth is, though, we don't have the luxury of choice in this matter and no one knows, for the most part, when or how their life will end. This applies to our loved ones, as well. Last year, my twenty-six-year-old son was out celebrating his birthday with friends when he stepped outside for a smoke and was hit by a flying fire hydrant dislodged by a speeding car. He hovered between life and death for three days before beginning his long and continuing recovery. He'll never be quite the same, but we still have him around to love. During the three days he was battling for his life, I felt that "scooped-out-soul" feeling I had experienced years ago, hovering around me, just waiting for an opportunity to overtake me. Only this time, it was for real.

My first near-death event didn't have a lasting effect on me. We were young. It happened quickly. We knew we were lucky, but life went on and it was soon forgotten.

The eighteen hours we spent trying to survive in the Atlantic Ocean definitely has stuck with me and has altered my approach to life. But God wasn't done yet. He had to smack me upside the head a third time to get my attention with my son's near death to really make an impression. I've always been a little thickheaded; it must be my German side. And, who knows... He may have to whack me again before it's all over. I get the feeling it's not a matter of if, but when.

I think the message in all this is simple and yet profound at the same time. What if we make the effort to appreciate all the wonderful things in our lives every day? Take a few minutes and thank God for all His blessings. I am thankful, every day, for all of the blessings in my life... from my family and friends, to a beautiful day on the water, and everything in between. When I find myself bogged down in less important worries and problems, all I have to do is think back to that night in the water when I was certain my life was over, or to the night my son almost lost his. It gives me the perspective I need to appreciate what I do have and not what I don't have. God doesn't always give us what we want, but He does provide us with what we need.

Dave and I share bonds that will last our lifetimes. We not only have a long-running friendship and share a love for fishing, but of course experienced our survival story together. Even more profoundly, we both experienced the near loss of a child. I can't even begin to explain the emotion involved with that..., just that it runs deep.

We retold our story many times over the next few months to family, friends and acquaintances and, each time, it felt like we were reliving it. Today, years later, it doesn't come up as often, but when I tell the story, it still always seems like it just happened yesterday. When I look at my beautiful daughter, Jessie, who wouldn't even be here; and Patrick, my grandson and best buddy, who would never have known me..., the tears roll freely at what we would have missed ... and at what we haven't missed, all at the same time.

I want to thank Dave for inviting me to help write this book and get my perspective of our misadventure out there. It has been bouncing around inside me for a long time, waiting to be let loose. It has been a blast. I also want to thank Chris Griggs for all her tireless work in typing, organizing, editing and her technical know-how. I have enjoyed all those Thursday nights we spent being the 'Nerd Herd', cleaning our glasses and sipping tea while working, along with all the laughs and giggles. Wherever this book goes, it has already been a success in my eyes. Peace and God Bless.

Arthur J. Higbee

COAST GUARD NEWS

NEW JERSEY

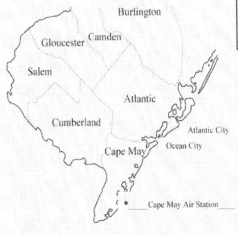

Burlington
Gloucester Camden
Salem
Atlantic
Cumberland
Atlantic City
Cape May
Ocean City
Cape May Air Station

At 7:30 AM a 41-foot utility boat from Great Egg and a helicopter from the air station Cape May responded and searched all day (see search pattern below)

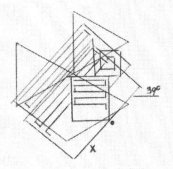

● Melvin H. Baker picked up three people from the water.

X US Coast Guard helicopter hoisted two people from the water.

THIRD COAST GUARD OPERATION CENTER

CASP ANALYSIS FOR

THE SUNKEN P/C HOT STUFF

CASE STUDY

<u>NARRATIVE</u>:   On Saturday, 14 September 1986, at about 0717Q, the P/C HOT STUFF sank with five men onboard. The vessel was believed to sink about 30 nautical miles Southeast of Ocean City, New Jersey. The details of the case are covered in the case study conducted by Coast Guard Group Cape May.

During the case, Group Cape May was in constant contact with the Third District Operation Center. When the initial searches were completed with negative results, the OPCEN opened a Computer Assisted Search Plan (CASP) to develop datum drift and future search areas. The initial CASP was opened at approximately 1400Q on the 14th. The CASP was run assuming two situations. The first was a disabled boat in the last known position. The second situation assumed the HOT STUFF had sunk and the POB were in the water. Both situations were drifted until 1600Q. The vessel situation drifted 6.1nm in the direction of 185T. The person in the water situation drifted 0.5nm in the direction of 180T. This information was used to plan the second and third searches.

Once the second and third searches turned up negative results, a second CASP was run. This run deleted the possibility of a vessel being adrift. The person in the water situation was drifted until 1900Q. The resulting datum drifted 0.65nm in the direction of 180T from the initial position passed by the HOT STUFF. This information helped generate the fourth search area.

<u>DISCUSSION</u>:   The basic assumptions used to run this CASP were correct. The most critical assumption was the position used for

the incident. This was the position passed by the HOT STUFF to Group Cape May. It was 118T and 11.2nm from the position Group Cape May estimated as the actual position of the incident after the survivors were debriefed. The inaccurate initial position ultimately caused the search areas generated by the CASP to be placed to the north of the position where the survivors were found.

The CASP was run with a position uncertainty of 5nm and a time uncertainty of 15 minutes. These assumptions were used due to the proximity of the incident to shore and the time the incident was reported. The uncertainty associated with these factors would not affect the final CASP datum drift. After the case was concluded, the CASP was run with position uncertainties of 10 nm and 15 nm. The resulting datums were slightly to the south of the datum which used 5nm as the position uncertainty.

Recently, CASP has added a reverse drift function. This can be used to calculate where an incident occurred knowing where survivors or debris are found. This function was used in the analysis of this case. The reverse drift was run assuming the survivors were swimming in the direction of 270T, plus or minus 45 degrees, at 0.5kts, plus or minus 0.5kts. The results were that the incident may have occurred at a position 007T, 4.3nm from the position the survivors were found. This is 278T, 6.2nm from the position Group Cape May calculated as the actual incident position.

CONCLUSIONS: Because of the short duration of this case, all the features of CASP were not used. The CASP decision aids were not needed due to the limited number of searches. However, the use of CASP for a short term offshore case was very beneficial. The entries needed to enter the program were quickly available and the resulting drift greatly assisted the search planners. Also, if the survivors had not been found, the report of the overdue vessel would have spurred further searches. Because CASP had already been accessed, the planning of the next day searches would have been much easier. All search planners should be aware of the benefits of CASP, even in the initial phases of a case.

The use of the reverse drift function of SASP seems to confirm

Group Cape May's calculation of the actual incident position. The difference with the CASP position and the Cape May estimated position can be accounted for by the uncertainty of the information from the survivors and the inaccuracies of the CASP drift factors. This helps confirm the usefulness of the reverse drift function. It can be used to calculate where an incident occurred once debris is found. The incident position would then be helpful to calculate the drift of a life raft.

REPORTED BY THE COAST GUARD: On Saturday, 14 September 1986, at 0717Q Coast Guard Group Cape May, NJ received a broken distress transmission on Channel 16 VHF-FM. The mayday was a single, continuous broadcast which was "stepped on" by other, stronger traffic in the area. The information which was ascertained by a quick study of the taped distress call was: a vessel with at least one male onboard was in distress. The vessel's reported position was 135 degrees, 20 miles from Ocean City and the length was believed to be 32 feet. The nature of distress, the number of people onboard and the amount and type of lifesaving / signaling devices were unknown. The name of the vessel was very garbled, but sounded like [HOT STUFF]. Whether the direction was 135 degrees true or 135 degrees magnetic was not stated and the distance was assumed to be in nautical miles vice statute miles. The point of reference, Ocean City, was determined to be Ocean City, New Jersey, vice Maryland, by telephone inquiries to Coast Guard units in those areas asking if they had heard a mayday.

At 0735Q, CG41344 (CG Station Great Egg NJ) and CG1389 (an HH52A from Coast Guard Station Cape May) were en-route positions approximately 135 degrees, 20 nautical miles from Ocean

City, NJ. The UTB went to a datum based on 135 degrees true and the helo went to one based on 135 degrees magnetic. At 0807Q, CG1389 inserted a data marker buoy and commenced a single-unit vector search with 10 mile track legs. At 0830Q, CG41344 commenced an expanding square search with 1 mile track spacing. No distressed vessel, survivors or debris were found. At 1015Q, an urgent marine broadcast was issued. At 1150Q, Coast Guard Station Great Egg had completed, with negative results, an ex comm. to determine if a vessel [HOT STUFF] was homeported in their area of responsibility. At 1156Q, CG41344 departed scene. There were three additional HH52A sorties flown. The first two searched a 10 by 16 mile area with 1 mile track spacing centered on a datum which was adjusted for drift. The last search covered a 6 by 8- mile area and was designed to be a quick search before dark in the most probable position as determined by CCGDTHREE CASP. At 2000Q the active search was suspended pending further developments. The lack of supporting information (no follow-up radio transmissions, no local knowledge of the boat, and no report of an overdue), the size of the area searched, completion of multiple searches in the area of highest probability, darkness, and the possibility that the case was a hoax or self-helped distress were all considered when requesting and receiving permission to suspend the search.

At 0040Q, on 15 September (17 hours after the mayday)the M/V MELVIN H. BAKER, a 555-foot bulk carrier, reported seeing and hearing three men in the water and they were coming about to assist. An HH52A was again dispatched. At 0118Q the BAKER reported they had recovered three men and heard, but couldn't find, two other men yelling in the darkness.

At 0135Q, the helo recovered the other two men. As the rescue was taking place, Coast Guard Station Great Egg reported they were taking information of an overdue vessel named HOT STUFF. All five men were treated for exposure and released from the hospital shortly before sunrise.

CONCLUSION: Seat cushions, coolers, jugs and five men in the water with a flare gun make a fair search target. The search weather was good. If the position was accurate, why didn't we find them?

It is believed that their transmitted position was approximately 10 miles off. The following was used to determine this:

a) The survivors said that approximately an hour after the HOT STUFF sank, they saw a Coast Guard helicopter coming directly at them, but it turned and headed south less than a quarter mile from them. The time, direction and turn coincide with the helicopter's actions at the end of the last leg of the initial pattern. The only turn which could have looked like this to the survivors was this turn. The last leg turn was 120 degrees true, 10nm from datum.

b) The survivors also stated they watched the helicopters all day methodically search back and forth to the west of them, coming closer, but always leaving before making it to them. They described all four helicopter sorties and said they never saw a helo to the east of them. This coincides with the rest of the days' search efforts if the men were drifting about 10nm to the SSE of datum.

c) The position where the BAKER found them was roughly "backtracked", using actual winds, predicted currents and considering the direction and speed of their swimming, to also fall approximately 10nm, SSE from the original datum.

d) Their destination, 60 miles, 135 degrees from Ocean City, New Jersey "sea buoy" was programmed into the HOT STUFF's LORAN "C" receiver at departure. The radio operator remembered seeing 135 degrees true 40nm to their destination on the display of the receiver an "undetermined" time before they were in trouble. With this he deduced that they were 135 degrees, 20 miles from their origin, Ocean

City. Two errors were introduced to the position with this deduction: 1) He used the "sea buoy's" position for programming, but transmitted simply "Ocean City" in the distress call. The "sea buoy" is approximately 2.5 miles offshore. 2) HOT STUFF was traveling southeast at 15 knots during this "undetermined" time. The radio operator remembered being relieved of the helm, putting on a full suit of foul weather gear and returning to stand beside the console in this time period. If this took him 30 minutes, HOT STUFF traveled 7.5 nautical miles. The combination of these two errors would explain the 10 miles difference.

Considering the above evidence, it is more likely than not that HOT STUFF was 135 degrees true, 30 nautical miles from Ocean City, NJ when she went down and thus was never in our search area.

SURVIVOR DEBRIEF: Five men left on HOT STUFF from Ocean City, New Jersey to fish for tuna in the canyon area, 60 miles from Ocean City. The HOT STUFF was a 1986, 32-foot, center console ocean racer with twin 200hp outboards. They were "running with the seas" at about 15mph when the HOT STUFF "surfed" to the bottom of a 4 to 6-foot wave where the bow was driven into the next wave (also about 4 to 6 feet high). The bow went under "for about five seconds and came up with a violent water spray." "The wall of water shattered the windshield and stalled the engines." They started to bail, but a wave broke over the low transom so they decided to start the engines and bow into the seas. That idea was abandoned when the next wave hit and they had water up to the gunwales. The mayday broadcast was started on Channel 68 VHF-FM, but it was switched to CH 16 where a complete distress message was broadcast before a wave hit the console and shorted the radio. The men donned Type III PFD's (which were blue in color), detached floating material (seat cushions, coolers, etc.) for a "debris slick" and assembled on the bow. They entered the water when the boat capsized. At 0742Q, they saw the bow of the HOT STUFF go under.

They fired one of three flares a few minutes after the boat sank and the other two when they saw the first Coast Guard helicopter. After the helo turned away not seeing the flares, they talked about how foolish it was to fire the flares "with the red sun at our backs and using the red flares, we realized it was impossible for the helicopter crew to see them."

They swam together until the two older men began to tire and slow down. An unplanned split occurred when the first group (of three) looked back and the other two men were gone.

At about 1600Q, the first group found and strapped themselves to what they believed to be a lobster pot buoy. They later moved to another buoy about a half-mile away where they planned to spend the night, hoping that a first-light search or the lobstermen would find them.

The three yelled in unison at a freighter passing within 50 yards. As the MELVIN H. BAKER launched their lifeboat, the first group heard their other two friends yelling in the distance. At one point, they actually saw them in the moonlight.

LESSONS LEARNED - THEIRS: The owner of HOT STUFF learned of EPIRBs after his rescue. If he would have known what an EPIRB was, and how relatively inexpensive they were, he said he would have had one onboard. In fact, he now believes they should be required equipment on vessels 26 feet in length or larger.

One survivor believed groin straps should be on all PFDs because, he said, "It was impossible to swim with my PFD up around my neck." He also wished he had worn a Type I or Type II PFD because he couldn't rest in his Type III. One felt blue PFDs should be outlawed because, "I felt so helpless waiving my arms and trying to be noticed while wearing a blue outfit." They all felt they would have drowned without them.

LESSONS LEARNED - OURS: HOT STUFF's distress call was "stepped on" by another vessel calling the Coast Guard. The caller was reporting the position of a disabled vessel (making it one of the more noble calls made to the Coast Guard on Channel 16), but it still interrupted an actual distress call. Technology has made it feasible for the average boater to monitor two VHF-FM frequencies. With the volume of traffic on our single distress and calling frequency, serious thought should be given to designating one frequency for calling and another for distress traffic. This would also improve the clarity of distress transmissions by clearing the airwaves to only emergency traffic. Until a permanent solution to this problem can be enacted, our radio watchstanders will continue to discourage the use of Channel 16 for radio checks and as a general information "hotline" to the Coast Guard.

AN ACCOUNTING IN

THE HISTORY OF THE MELVIN H. BAKER

The following is a section of the history of the *Melvin H. Baker* as recorded by the National Gypsum History (http://ngc-heritage.com/op-ships-baker.htm).

All of the Baker crews were Chinese and its first captain, Peter Thomas Chow, was married on board. In September, 1986, the ship made a rescue at sea. This is the account from a company publication, "People to People:"

Had it not been for the calm weather conditions shortly after midnight on Sept. 15 this year (1986), Captain Lin and his crew would never have rescued five men from drowning. Two fishing boats, an oil tanker and a bulk carrier had already passed the men, unable to hear their cries for help.

The water-logged boaters had been in the ocean near Cape May, NJ, since 7 a.m. when their speedboat, the Hot Stuff, raced over a swell, nose-dived into the water and sank. For more than eighteen hours, three men hung onto a red float, while the others drifted nearby. Each wore a flotation jacket.

"It scared me to hear the cries for help so close," Captain Lin said. "At first, I thought there was a man overboard, but I quickly realized my crewmen would have called for help in Chinese."

The crew determined approximately from where the sounds were coming. Then they circled and ran the same course, starting and stopping the engine to avoid machinery noise.

When the crew heard three of the men about two or three hundred feet away, they turned on the spotlights and notified the Coast Guard. A lifeboat was lowered and the shivering boaters were pulled from the ocean.

"The chance of hearing their cries was very, very slim. If they had been on the other side of the ship, we would have never heard them because the wind would have carried the sound away from us. Those men were very lucky."

Although not mentioned by the captain in his history report, it is important to mention that the *Melvin H. Baker* was one of the ships searching for the vessel *Andrea Gail*, which was lost at sea during the 'storm of the century' in October 1991, as mentioned in the book, *The Perfect Storm*, by Sebastian Junger.

There is no way of knowing how the men on the *Andrea Gail* actually reacted during that storm, since there were no survivors to tell the tale in truth. This book, however, is a true and actual accounting of what happened to the boat *Hot Stuff* and to its crew and their reactions as the realization of certain death set in on the morning of September 15, 1986 when their vessel sank.

ABOUT THE AUTHORS

Daniel David Jones (left and better known as "Dave") was born and raised in South Jersey where he still resides with his wife, Barbara, and five children: Lisa, Laura, Lynn, Daniel and David. He is a union carpenter and is still a die-hard fisherman who loves his family and life. He has shared his story at churches and family retreats from coast to coast. The short story version of *Promising Forecast* has been published in five major magazines and Outdoor Life Networks re-enacted a segment on their *"This Happened To Me"* television series.

Arthur J. Higbee (right and better known as "Art") was born in Jamaica, Queens, New York and moved to Northfield, New Jersey, in the late 1950's where he still lives today with his wife, Anna, and children Joe and Jessie. He is a practicing chiropractor and continues to fish, surf and enjoy all the available water activities he can, now sharing them with not only his children, but also with his grandson, Patrick, his best buddy.

Made in the USA
Charleston, SC
31 January 2016